the Wit & Wisdom of the Talmud

Proverbs, Sayings *and* Parables *for the* Ages

edited by

George J. Lankevich

SQUAREONE
CLASSICS

Cover Designer: Phaedra Mastrocola
Typesetter: Gary A. Rosenberg
Series Consultant: Skip Whitson
In-House Editor: Joanne Abrams
Printer: Paragon Press, Honesdale, PA

Square One Publishers
Garden City Park, NY 11040
(516) 535–2010
www.squareonepublishers.com

Library of Congress Cataloging-in-Publication Data
Talmud. English. Selections.
    The wit and wisdom of the Talmud : proverbs, sayings, and parables for
the ages / edited by George J. Lankevich.
        p. cm. — (Squareone classics)
Includes index.
        ISBN 0-7570-0021-5 (pbk.)
        1. Talmud—Quotations. 2. Proverbs, Jewish—Translations into
English. 3. Talmud—Parables. I. Lankevich, George J., 1939- II.
Title. III. Series.
        BM495 .T3 2002
        296.1'250521—dc21

                                                                                2001004158

Square One Classics is an imprint of Square One Publishers, Inc.

Printed in the United States of America

10   9   8   7   6   5   4   3   2   1

Contents

Introduction, 1

Topics

Introduction

The history of the Jewish people is an unending adventure story, a chronicle that has inspired Western thought for millennia. It is a saga of wandering and enslavement, promise and persecution, tragedy and achievement. During the course of forty centuries, enormous cultural contributions have been made by individual Jewish men and women in every field of human activity. But most importantly, the Hebraic search for meaning has given humankind two of its most profound literary creations—the Old Testament of the Bible and those rabbinic interpretations and debates that form the Talmud. The wisdom and learning that can be obtained from the Talmud is the subject of the pages that fill this volume.

The Old Testament details the long spiritual quest of the Jewish nation, an unfolding of the covenantal relationship between God and his chosen people. The Torah (Pentateuch), which comprises the first five books of the Bible, establishes the laws and teachings that men and women must follow in order to please and placate an all-knowing and all-powerful Creator. Since the expectations of the Almighty are eternal, and His wisdom forever, it can even be said that the Torah existed before Creation itself. Since the books of the Torah proclaim the special relationship between God and the Hebrew people, and contain the essence of Judaism, an ancient Babylonian tradition asserts that God Himself spends the first three hours of each day perusing it. Moses, who probably lived in the thirteenth century BCE, was the Hebrew chief who received the Torah (law or instruction) from God on Mount Sinai. He is the primary human figure of the Pentateuch, but he is surely not the author of its books in any literal sense. Rather he was the conduit through which God's commands came to men, and his authoritative teachings provided the stimulus for the formal compilation of the Torah almost seven centuries before the Common Era began.

It is important to understand that the teachings of Moses, the Law that the Almighty made known as the prophet led his people in the trackless wastes of the Sinai Desert, really belong to all nations. To Jews, the texts of the Pentateuch are sacred—divine commands that are the core of their belief system, words that mandate the will of God throughout all time. The eternal value of the Law is demonstrated by the reverence given to the scrolls of leather or parchment on which the books of the Pentateuch are inscribed, the Torah within the ark that is used in the synagogue during services. Every Jew struggles to protect and to understand the Torah. Such study (Talmud) takes as one of its principles that since the Torah "was published in the open desert, it is the property of the whole world; everyone is at liberty to assume the responsibilities it imposes." The Torah belongs to all humanity.

A Religion of the Law

Judaism is fundamentally a religion of Law and obligation. Rabbis who study and define the requirements of the Jewish faith must consult not only the written Torah, but also an ancient "Oral Tradition" that interprets the commandments given to Moses. Study in the academies of the ancient world was conducted orally, yet the insights gained by plumbing the rich meanings of the words of God were not to be lost or discarded. Gradually, a body of wisdom was created to give direction in daily existence. Jews came to consider the Torah and its manifold commentaries to be of divine origin; both equally bind observant Jews. The sages who have labored since the days of Moses to explain the divine words perform an essential task, and they have the rare privilege of living a scholarly existence not possible for most Jews. Yeshivas provide the contemporary setting where study is performed by dedicated students, yet all individuals have an obligation to study the Law as best they can. Every person has the capability of adding an original thought to Talmudic wisdom, and it is clear that the amount of Torah knowledge on Earth is constantly increasing as study proceeds. The message that informs the efforts of every Talmudic scholar is crystal clear: "Every house a temple, every heart an altar, every human being a priest."

To study the Torah and the Talmud is to participate in and experience the divine will, to discover the manner in which people should live under God's Law. Jews believe that adherence to the Law will insure the cultural and religious survival of their nation, but they have always been eager to debate the exact nature of God's commands. To contemplate, to analyze, to discuss the meaning of the Law and define its requirements can become the work of a scholarly lifetime; it is a pursuit so serious and meaningful that it has elicited the most creative efforts of each generation since Moses. The Talmud, quoted so freely in this book, is the product of thousands of minds and countless hours of study. Indeed, the word Talmud is most often translated as simply "study." People can best honor God by abiding by His eternal laws, as well as their poor brains can understand these timeless yet ever-debated injunctions. Talmudic study is perhaps the greatest living heritage of Classical Judaism, a vocation that is still vital despite a world that becomes increasingly secular.

The Evolution of the Talmud

From the time of Moses, Jewish scholars passed on oral learning to their willing students. The written Law of the Torah was thus reinforced by both oral teaching and written directives, and all merged into a living reality that infused the daily life of the Jews. Thus, the Jews lived under rules interpreted by successive generations of scholars who sought to inform and inspire an often difficult and almost always contentious people. The most vital and complete of these codes was the Mishnah, a collection of oral rules presented in Hebrew that explained the scriptural Torah laws. The Gemara offered commentaries on and elaborations of the Mishnah, but these were largely presented in Aramaic, the common language of the time. Both the Mishnah and the Gemara were supplemented by a range of auxiliary materials from other than Palestinian sources. Creating a single version of the Talmud from this vast welter of commentary and material would be the work of centuries, involve an untold number of dedicated scholars, and produce competing versions of the work before a standard version was accepted. No one really knows when *Talmud* became the preferred word to describe these commentaries. The most probable sequence is as follows.

During the First Temple Era (950–586 BCE), many teachers followed the example of Moses and instructed the Jews in the expectations of God. Among them, and the first to be named in the Bible, was the high priest Ezra, who "prepared his heart to expound the Torah of God and to do and to teach among the people of Israel law and justice." Ezra read the Torah before the nation, and explained its mandates to an attentive people. Because of such efforts, a code of conduct—rules for proper Jewish life—existed before the return of the Jews from their Babylonian Captivity in 586 BCE. By the end of the Second Jewish Commonwealth (586 BCE–70 CE), examinations of the Torah had expanded into sixty-three long treatises, which were conveyed to future generations primarily by rabbinical memory and repetition. The rabbis had thus created an "oral Torah," one consisting of traditions passed on until they were given written form in the body of knowledge called the Mishnah.

The treatises of the Mishnah are grouped into six great "orders" (sedarim), or divisions, each of which focuses on a specific issue. The eleven treatises of rules concerning Agriculture/Seeds (Zeraim) cover tithes, first fruits, sacrifices, and gifts due from the produce of the land; the cessation of agricultural labor during the Sabbatical year; and prohibited mixtures in seeds and grafting. Feasts/Observances (Moed) deals with the Sabbath and Sabbath rest; feasts such as Passover, Tabernacles, and the New Year; and fasts. It details work forbidden, ceremonies to be observed, and sacrifices to be made on those days. Women (Nashim), the shortest of the sedarim, presents legislation concerning marriage, divorce, adultery, and vows. Damages/Fines (Nezikin) covers civil and criminal law as related to commercial transactions, purchases, sales, mortgages, legal procedures, the organization of tribunals, witnesses, and oaths, as well as a brief on idolatry and a collection of the ethical sentences of the rabbis. Sacred Things (Kodoshim) provides a detailed description of Herod's Temple, and discusses laws that regulate temple sacrifices, donations, the first born, and clean and unclean animals. Lastly, Purification (Taharot) presents regulations concerning the purity of vessels, dwellings, foods, and persons, and specific rituals of purification. Consisting of twelve treatises, the Purification section is long and involved.

So great was Mishnah's importance that every word and every phrase deserved to be analyzed and discussed in all possible permutations. Only when all possibilities had been covered did the rabbinical consideration move on to the next part. The learned commentary was often extensive, and discussion became so complex that erudition often seemed to replace the words of Mishnah. Because of the complexity of the commentary, there were inevitably lapses of memory as the discussion progressed. Differences abounded, nuances were lost, and after hundreds of years there were as many versions of the Mishnah as there were teachers (tannaim). But both the "oral Torah" and the commentaries upon its meaning were vital parts of the faith transmitted from Moses.

During the time that Jesus Christ was alive in Palestine, the most important schools of interpretation involved followers of the influential Rabbis Hillel and Shammai. Both were Pharisees—members of a sect that emphasized adherence to the laws of purity—and both of their lives extended into the first years of the Common Era. But the scholars differed greatly on such legal matters as the Mishnah regulations regarding purity and Sabbath observation. Both men devoutly pondered the laws, customs, and institutions of Judaism, and gradually, over the course of the first century, the school of Hillel attained more authority. Even today, Hillel's advice to a non-Jew who wished to study Jewish law is widely quoted. "Do not unto others that which you would not have them do to you. That is the entire Torah. The rest is commentary. Now go and study." But exactly what to study remained uncertain and led to the compilation of a single version of the Mishnah. It was the genius of Judah ha-Nasi (135–220 CE), sometimes called The Prince or The Patriarch, that successfully brought all competing versions of the

Mishnah into agreement. Out of the mass of oral traditions and written judgments, he produced a single accepted format around 200 CE. His work was striking in that it rarely justified itself by quoting scripture, but it succeeded in formalizing the content of the Mishnah. Texts that The Prince excluded as insufficiently authoritative or repetitious were declared "external" parts of the Mishnah, but most were collected by rabbis in Babylon into an "Addition" (Tosefta), which they used in their studies.

Because of Judah ha-Nasi, an agreed-upon Mishnah now existed that codified the oral teachings of a millennium. In the centuries that followed Judah's achievement, two geographically separated groups of Jewish scholars (amoraim)—the first in Palestine and the second in Babylon—labored to explain the text of the Mishnah and to clarify and reconcile apparent areas of contradiction. But common approaches to language and law proved elusive because of rivalry between the two schools. The words of the Mishnah were Hebrew, the language of the scholars was Aramaic, and considerations of prestige divided the scholars. Both groups understood that none of the oral tradition could be discarded, being as vital as Torah itself, but competing rabbis gave advice according to the circumstances of their own age, adding a huge amount of material to the Mishnah. These new amoraim never disputed the rulings of previous tannaim, but refashioned the Law to fit the changing circumstances of the Jewish people. Their efforts produced a vast new store of commentary known as the Gemara—a maze of judgments, rendered in Aramaic, that had to be incorporated into the growing Talmud. It is not surprising to learn that both Gemara (Aramaic) and Talmud (Hebrew) mean study.

The Gemara comments on the Mishnah, just as the Mishnah comments on the Torah. One version of the Gemara, the work of Palestine scholars in Galilee and often inaccurately identified as the Jerusalem Talmud, was edited in Tiberas about 380 CE. The Jerusalem Talmud was brief and coherent, but even today there is no scholarly agreement on its text. Continued uncertainty regarding the text of the Jerusalem Talmud inspired greater effort in Babylon, and over the course of the next century, a larger, more authoritative Talmud was compiled by rabbis at Sura. In approximately 500 CE, Rav Ashi and his colleagues produced the much larger Babylonian Talmud (Bavli), a work that immediately attained intellectual primacy because it was compiled with full knowledge of the Palestinian rabbis. Literate, clear, and logical, the Babylonian Talmud contains 2.5 million words and is three times the size of the Palestine Talmud. Incorporating long scriptural passages to buttress its arguments, the Babylonian Talmud offers a vast "ocean" of learning and much deeper documentation for its positions. Its depth and complexity attract the modern Orthodox scholar as surely as a magnet does iron. The rulings of literally hundreds of amoraim are mentioned in a text that provides the basis for Jewish life in a harsh and often uncaring world. The Babylonian Talmud is considered to be the most significant effort at explaining the complexities of living under the Torah, a position it has held for over fifteen centuries. It is more complete and more studied, more copied and commented upon than its earlier rival. Moreover, we have far more authoritative versions of its text. Although modern libraries have handwritten parts of Talmuds dating to the eighth century, our earliest complete manuscripts date from the thirteenth (Jerusalem) and fourteenth (Babylonian) centuries. No reasonable scholar believes that there was a single "original text" of either, and neither exists today in a version accepted by everyone.

The Talmud In Medieval Times

Since the Torah is the word of God, His fundamental rules of living, it is hardly surprising that more than 70 percent of the Jerusalem Talmud and fully half of the Babylonian Talmud revolved around legal obligations. Yet so vast was the body of rabbinical analysis that neither compilation completely examined all of the Mishnah. For example, both Talmuds skirted issues of purification. To live according to the will of God is the highest aspiration of every Jew, and the goal of Talmudic study has always been to make clear the path towards goodness, but the complex Law often appeared to contain exceptions as well as contradictions.

Moreover, the Talmud's concerns ranged far beyond legal obligations. After the sixth century, those rabbis who commented on the Talmud were called seburaim (opinionists), and their weighty judgments (halakhah) attempted to cover virtually every aspect of daily life. Ordinary folk constantly consulted scholars to seek personal advice, because the rabbis' dedication to study made them the natural leaders of the community. Over time, new information, rules, and subjects of interest to the people and to their rabbis made their way into the Talmud. Its range of concerns expanded to incorporate commercial advisories, travel arrangements, tales of Alexander the Great, lessons in astronomy, and advice about professions (for every rabbi had a job), as well as rules of civil, criminal, and dietary law. It is the almost infinite variety of the Talmud that has over the ages drawn historians, antiquarians, ethnologists, scientists, preachers, lawyers, artisans, housewives, humorists, and philosophers. Far more than a legal tome, it became a compendium of all human experience.

As another five centuries passed, scores of different contributors made additions to the Talmud, superimposing complex layer upon complex layer. Once again a search for order was inevitable, and in the Middle Ages, a series of great commentators gave renewed coherence to the Talmud. Today's twelve folio volumes preserve the labors of Jewish teachers from medieval days to our own. Among the greatest of these scholars was Sholomo Yitzchaki of Troyes (Rashi) (1045–1105), who during the eleventh century produced the first great analysis of the Babylonian Talmud in pure Hebrew. Rashi attempted to anticipate the difficulties facing future students, and laid out rabbinical procedure in minute detail and nuance. His goal was not innovation but rather common sense and the conservation of tradition. The Spanish scholar Moses Maimonides (1135–1204) commented on the Mishnah in the late twelfth century, and his *Mishne Torah (The Torah Reviewed)* was used by Moses ben Nahman

(Ramban) (1194–1270), Solomon ben Adret (Rashba) (1235–1310), and Nissim ben Reuben Gerondi (Ran). Each of these scholars worked from the Babylonian version of the Talmud and helped to validate its primacy. Each also wrote Aggadah (narratives) that added to the complexity of Talmud study. The continuing relevance of such study was demonstrated as Jewish communities in diverse areas of Europe retained the essence of their faith under vastly different circumstances. A virtual library of wisdom was being created to offer reasonable answers to life's myriad problems.

Throughout history, enemies of the Jews have attempted to halt the study of the Talmud. In 1242, for example, over twenty carts filled with Talmudic manuscripts were burnt in Paris by Catholic fanatics, and many other copies were destroyed in Italy during the Counter Reformation of the sixteenth century. Talmuds were burned in Poland in 1757 during a persecution of the Jews, and the Nazis of modern Germany made the Talmud a target of opportunity before they attempted to annihilate the Jews themselves. But no effort succeeded in eliminating its presence. Both a complete manuscript copy of the Palestinian Talmud dating back to the thirteenth century and a handwritten copy of its Babylonian version from the next century exist. And almost as much as Jewish scholars, Christian sages have always turned to the Talmud to better understand the origins of their faith. As medieval times drew towards a close, the first mass printing of the Babylonian Talmud began in Catholic Spain (1482). Pope Leo X approved the first complete editions of both Talmuds in Venice (1520–1523), yet it was Pope Julius XII who ordered the destruction of all existing copies a generation later (1553). But regardless of the Christian world's view of the Talmud, the text became widely circulated. Over one hundred editions were published before the Vilnus edition of the Babylonian Talmud of 1886 became the generally accepted standard version.

The Lasting Value of the Talmud

The Talmud has been a vital force in Jewish life for over 1,500 years. The Law is a gift from the Almighty, and the many attempts to clarify its meaning represent not only immense scholarship, but also common sense and folk wisdom. To study the Talmud is a calling, a mission, a lifetime of pleasure. Study itself is a kind of religious rite, a vocation that brings personal joy and piety. It constantly returns the Jewish people to their Biblical roots; they cling to the Torah, learn from the Talmud, and attempt to live in a manner pleasing to God. Yet it is vital to understand that the Talmud's value is universal. An old Jewish axiom promises that the righteous of all nations will have a portion in the future world, so it seems only right to offer Talmudic advice to a world that seems at times to have lost its moral compass. Noble ideals and exalted ideas may be found in many places, but the Talmud—which has served as a daily guide for countless people over so many centuries—seems uniquely suited to point the way toward a happier life.

Indeed, much of the Talmud's wisdom is already very much a part of general consciousness. "Birds of a feather flock together" and "Actions speak louder than words" are just two of the adages that come to us from the Talmud. Many of its insights have been recast in different words to fit the needs of other cultures, but they continue to show their Talmudic roots. Our selection from the "ocean" of wisdom that emerged from Talmudic study is merely a taste of the common sense found within its pages. In a rushed and challenging world, the quiet life of the scholar seems "wasted." Yet the adages, proverbs, and judgments drawn from study and contemplation can provide a foundation for a compassionate and focused life. Although seemingly commonplace and familiar, these words present ideals that are not impossible to achieve—merely difficult because they demand so much. Rabbis have long studied the Law of God and the duties of the Jews, but they assumed that all men are equal; all share in the image of the Creator. All people live in the world He provided, and each has a responsibility towards other people and that world. All belong to families, fight evil inclinations, and repent of the inevitable failings that arise out of our common nature. Meditating on humankind's common heritage can help every individual's personal search for meaning and goodness. If these excerpts from the Talmud inspire a single person, they will have accomplished the dream of millennia.

The Wit & Wisdom
of the Talmud

ACCOUNTABILITY

Consider three things and thou wilt never sin: remember
whence thou comest, whither thou goest, and before
whom thou wilt have to render an account for thy doings.

• ◆ •

Consider three things, and thou wilt never fall into sin:
remember that there is above thee an All-Seeing Eye,
an All-Hearing Ear, and a record of all thy actions.

• ◆ •

The end does not justify the means.

ACTIONS

Actions speak louder than words.

• ◆ •

He who performs a single good action gains for himself
an Advocate, and he who commits a single sin
procures for himself an Accuser.

• ◆ •

If thou hast commenced a good action,
leave it not incomplete.

$\mathcal{D}$o as much or little as thou canst,
only let thy intention be always good.

• ◆ •

$\mathcal{J}$udge a man by his deeds, not by his words.

• ◆ •

$\mathcal{T}$hy own deeds make thy friends or thy enemies.

• ◆ •

$\mathcal{A}$ tree is known by its fruit, so man by his works.

• ◆ •

$\mathcal{L}$et every man watch his own doings that he may be
an example to his fellow man through life.

• ◆ •

$\mathcal{T}$he action of a fool cannot serve as a precedent.

• ◆ •

$\mathcal{T}$he right way for man to choose is to do that which
is honorable in his own eyes and at the same time
honorable in the eyes of his fellow men.

ADVERSITY

$\mathcal{A}$dversity is the true school of the mind.

• ◆ •

$\mathcal{W}$hen the ox is down, many are the butchers.

DVICE

*H*ear sixty advisers, but be guided
by your own conviction.

• ◆ •

*F*ollow the counsel of the aged,
but act not upon the advice of the young.

• ◆ •

*B*eware of him who gives thee advice
according to his own interests.

• ◆ •

*I*t is an act of gracious manners on the part of
an important man to invite the counsel of a lesser.

• ◆ •

*P*oor servants ask advice after a thing has happened.

GE

*F*our things cause a man to age prematurely:
a fright, anger, children, and an evil-tempered wife.

• ◆ •

*H*appy is our old age if it atones for our youth.

How welcome is old age! The aged are beloved by god.

• ◆ •

Old men sometimes dye their hair,
but its roots remain white.

• ◆ •

Support the aged without reference to religion;
respect the learned without reference to age.

• ◆ •

To the aged man a small mound is comparable
to a tall mountain.

• ◆ •

To what may he be compared who learns from the aged?
To one who eats ripe grapes and drinks old wine.

• ◆ •

The old have no taste;
the young have no power of counsel.

 NCESTRY

He who has no inner nobleness has nothing,
even if he be of noble birth.

• ◆ •

No one partakes of the enjoyments of the
World to Come because of his father's merits.

The proverb runs: of what good is good birth
to a man of evil deeds.

ANGER

Anger profiteth nobody.

All men of anger are fools.

All men of anger are men of pride.

A sage who indulges in anger loses his knowledge.

Avoid anger and thou wilt not sin.

Anger showeth the character of a man.

The angry man's speech is like the water
which overflows from a boiling kettle.

The beginning of anger is madness,
the end penitence.

He who gives way to his wrath makes desolate his house.

• ◆ •

A man may be known by three things:
by his conduct in money matters, his behavior at the table
and his demeanor when angry.

• ◆ •

Be not easily moved to anger.

• ◆ •

To him who curbs his wrath, his sins will be forgiven.

• ◆ •

He who is slow to anger and easily pacified
is truly pious and virtuous.

• ◆ •

If in anger the one hand remove thy wife or thy child,
let the other hand again bring them back to thy heart.

• ◆ •

Three men are beloved by god: he who does not
become angry; he who does not become drunken;
and he who does not stand on his dignity.

APPEARANCES ARE DECEIVING

A penny in an empty box rattles loudly.

Two pieces of coin in one bag
make more noise than a hundred.

•—•

Look not at the cask, but at what is in it.
A new cask may contain old wine,
and an old one may be altogether empty.

•—•

One learned, who is not inwardly as outwardly,
is not to be looked upon as learned.

•—•

The dog follows thee, but his attachment is to
the crumb which he expects of thee.

•—•

When the castle goes to ruin, castle is still its name;
when the dunghill rises, still it is a dunghill.

ARROGANCE AND PRIDE

Arrogance is a kingdom without a crown.

•—•

A proud man is not acceptable
even in his own household.

Pride is like idolatry.

• ◆ •

The prayers of the proud are never heard.

• ◆ •

Pride leads to the destruction of man.

• ◆ •

Pride is a sign of the worst poverty—ignorance.

• ◆ •

The proud are pettish and the pettish are foolish.

• ◆ •

He who hardens his heart with pride
softens his brain with the same.

• ◆ •

The Messiah will not come until haughtiness
shall have ceased among men.

• ◆ •

It requires but the slightest breeze of ill-luck
to cast down the proud.

• ◆ •

What is the sign of a proud man?
He never praises anyone.

ASSOCIATES

Associate not with the wicked man,
even if thou canst learn from him.

• ◆ •

Ever associate with the good.

• ◆ •

If thy associates be insane, be thou sensible.

• ◆ •

He who consorts with immoral
people is himself immoral.

• ◆ •

Every beast associates with his own kind,
but man only with his equal.

• ◆ •

A man without a fitting companion
is like the left hand without the right.

• ◆ •

Not without reason goes the crow to the raven,
but because it is of its kind.

If you touch pitch, it will stick to your fingers;
even so, if you associate with evil companions,
you will acquire their vices.

• ◆ •

*W*hen the iron was created the trees commenced to
tremble. The iron, however, said to them:
"What are you trembling at? If none of your wood
will join me, I will remain harmless."

• ◆ •

*W*hen the flood came over the earth, and everything was
threatened with destruction, and every kind of beast in
pairs came to Noah, the Lie, too, asked admittance into
the ark. Noah, however, refused. "Only pairs may enter
here," he said. The Lie went in search of a companion, and
at last met Vice, whom it invited to go to the ark. "I am
willing to keep company with thee, if though wilt promise
to give me all thy earnings," said Vice. The Lie agreed, and
they were both admitted into the ark. After they left the
ark the Lie regretted her agreement, and wished to dissolve
partnership with Vice; but it was too late, and thus is it
current, that "what Lie earneth, Vice consumeth."

BEGINNINGS

*A*ll beginnings are difficult.

BIRTH AND DEVELOPMENT

Man enters and departs from the world
with loud outcries.

• ◆ •

There are three partners in man:
God, his father, and his mother.

• ◆ •

A man's life has three periods: the period when his body
develops; the period when his thought develops;
and the period when his deeds develop.

BUSINESS PRINCIPLES

It is not the amount of trade that makes the man
poor or rich, but honest working and dealing.

• ◆ •

A man cannot deny a debt in the face of his creditor.

• ◆ •

Credit and mutual trust should be the foundation of
commercial intercourse.

$\mathcal{G}$o to bed without supper, but rise without debt.

• ◆ •

If you have taken of a man his plough or his pillow
for debt, return his plough in the morning
and his pillow at night.

• ◆ •

$\mathcal{N}$ever take the clothes of wife or children
in payment of a debt.

• ◆ •

$\mathcal{T}$he possessions of a widow, whether she be rich or poor,
should not be taken in pawn.

• ◆ •

$\mathcal{H}$e who lends without interest is more worthy than he
who gives to charity; he who invests money in the
business of a poor man is most praiseworthy.

• ◆ •

If thy business does not prosper in one town try another.

• ◆ •

"$\mathcal{H}$e performed no evil against his fellow man,"
namely he began no competitive enterprise or trade
where there was no demand for it.

• ◆ •

$\mathcal{K}$eep partners with him whom the hour favors.

Rab Safra had a jewel for which he asked the price of ten pieces of gold. Several dealers saw the jewel and offered five gold pieces. Rab Safra declined, and the merchants left him. After a second consideration, he, however, resolved upon selling the jewel for five pieces. The next day, just as Rab Safra was at prayers, the merchants unexpectedly returned: "Sir," said they to him, "we come to you again to do business after all. Do you wish to part with the jewel for the price we offered you?" But Rab Safra made no reply. "Well, well; be not angered; we will add another two pieces." Rab Safra still remained silent. "Well, then, be it as you say; we will give you ten pieces, the price you asked." By this time Rab Safra had ended his prayer, and said, "Sirs, I was at prayers, and could not hear you. As for the jewel, I have already resolved upon selling it at the price you offered me yesterday. If you then pay me five pieces of gold, I shall be satisfied."

CHARACTER AND REPUTATION

The one great requisite is character.

The fool sees but the outer garment of a person; the wise man sees his inner garment—his character.

There are three crowns: that of the Law, the priesthood,
and royalty; but the crown of a good name
is loftier than all these.

• ◆ •

The most worthy crown is a good reputation.

• ◆ •

Three names are given to a man: one by his parents,
another by the world, and the third by his works—the one
which is written in the immortal book of his fate. Which of
these three names is the best? Solomon teaches us, when
he says: "A good name is better than the sweetest oil."

• ◆ •

Rather be thou the tail among lions
than the head among foxes.

• ◆ •

The ideal man has the strength of a male
and the compassion of a female.

CHARITY AND GOOD DEEDS

Charity is the salt of riches.

• ◆ •

Charity is the greatest virtue.

Charity is more than sacrifices.

• ◆ •

Good deeds are better than creeds.

• ◆ •

He that feeds the hungry feeds God also.

• ◆ •

He who does charity and justice is as if he had
filled the whole world with kindness.

• ◆ •

He who gives charity in secret is greater than Moses.

• ◆ •

He who stints on charity, deserves life
neither in this world nor the next.

• ◆ •

He who turns away from the works of love and charity,
turns away from God.

• ◆ •

If you see a man donating much to charity,
be assured that his wealth is increasing.

• ◆ •

It is permitted to do good to a man
without consulting him.

*L*et a man be generous in his charities,
but let him beware of giving away all that he has.

• ◆ •

A rabbi saw a man give a zuz to a beggar publicly.
He said to him, "Better you had given him nothing
than to give him and put him to shame."

• ◆ •

*T*he practice of beneficence will assure the
maintenance of one's possessions.

• ◆ •

*O*ur kindly deeds and our generous gifts go to Heaven as
messengers, and plead for us before our heavenly Father.

• ◆ •

*T*he merit of charitable works is in proportion
to the grace with which they are practiced.

• ◆ •

*T*he noblest of all charities is in enabling the poor
to earn a livelihood.

• ◆ •

*I*t is better to lend than to give.
To give employment is better than either.

• ◆ •

*L*end to the poor in the time of their need.

Charity is more valuable than sacrifices,
and alone equals the exercise of all religious forms.

• ◆ •

As a garment is made up of single threads,
so every single gift aids in building
the great work of charity.

• ◆ •

It is our duty to relieve the poor and the needy,
to visit the sick and bury the dead
without distinction of race or creed.

• ◆ •

Whosoever engages in the study of the Law,
and does not practice benevolence,
is to be compared to a man who has no God.

• ◆ •

Spending alms and practicing benevolence exceed
in importance all the other laws of the Torah.

• ◆ •

He gives little who gives with a frown.
He gives much who gives little with a smile.

• ◆ •

The world stands on three things:
on Law, Labor, and Benevolence.

To one that has the means but withholds relief
from the needy, God says; "Keep in mind
that it is I who made him poor and you rich;
I can also send reverses on thee
and make thee poor and him rich."

• ◆ •

Iron breaks stone; fire melts iron; water extinguishes fire;
the clouds consume water; the storm dispels clouds;
man withstands the storm; fear conquers man;
wine banishes fear; sleep overcomes wine;
and death is the master of sleep;
but "Charity," says Solomon,
"saves from death."

• ◆ •

Four dispositions are found among those who bestow
charity. There is he who is willing to give, but does not
wish others to give: he has an envious eye towards others.
There is he who wishes others to give, but who will not
give himself: he has an evil eye towards himself.
He who is willing to give and wishes others to give also,
is a pious man. He who neither gives himself
nor wishes others to give, is a wicked man.

• ◆ •

Blessed is he who gives from his substance to the poor;
twice blessed is he who accompanies his gift
with kind, comforting words.

Almsgiving is practiced by means of money,
but charity also by personal services and by words of advice,
sympathy, and encouragement. Almsgiving is a duty
towards the poor only, but charity towards the rich
as well as the poor, nay, even towards the dead.

• ◆ •

Man possesses three sorts of friends in this world: his
children, his wealth, and his Good Works.

In the hour of death he calls his children to his bedside:
"Oh, save me from the pangs of death," he cries. And the
afflicted children say: "Thou knowest, dear father, that
nothing can prevail against death; neither children, nor
relatives, nor friends are able to save man from death."
The Divine Word has gone forth: "Go, sleep in peace,
and prepare thyself for the day of judgment."

Then the dying man thinks of his wealth and calls it
to his assistance: "Oh, save me from that terrible sentence
of death." And his wealth answers him: "Gold and jewels
are powerless in the hour of God's wrath; the Divine Word
has proclaimed it."

Whereupon the dying man calls his Good Works and
says to them: "Oh, save me from the horrors of the pains
of death; leave me not to myself; come accompany me and
save me, for I was always your friend." And the Good
Works answer: "Depart in peace, good friend! Even before
you arrive there for judgment, we will have already reached
that place; for the Divine Word has gone forth to man:
'Thy virtue precedes thee on the way, even till heavenly
bliss receives thee.'"

One day the Roman Governor, T. Annius Rufus, asked Rabbi Akiba, "If your God loves the poor among the Hebrews, why does He not support them?" "Because God desires to give the rich an opportunity of doing good," was the Rabbi's reply. "How do you know," Rufus rejoined, "that this virtue of charity pleases God, since no master can be pleased, if a person aids a slave, whom he has seen fit to deprive of food and clothing?" "Even so," said Akiba; "but if the king, for some offense, had deprived his son of food and drink, and a person had prevented the prince from dying of hunger, would the king be wroth with that person? Certainly not, neither will God be displeased with those who dispense charity to His children, even to the fallen and the sinful."

HILDREN

*D*o not confine your children to your own learning, for they were born in another time.

• ◆ •

*I*f thou must strike a child, strike it with the string of a shoe.

• ◆ •

*T*he world itself rests upon the breath of children in the schoolhouse.

Do not threaten a child. Either punish or forgive him.

•—◆—•

A man appreciates the love of his grandchildren
more than the love of his children.

•—◆—•

The daughter is as the mother was.

•—◆—•

A good tree brings good fruit.

•—◆—•

What the child says out of doors he has learnt in doors.

•—◆—•

Parental love should be impartial;
one child must not be preferred to the other.

•—◆—•

It is a father's duty not only to provide for his minor
children, but also to take care of their instruction,
and to teach his son a trade and whatever
is necessary for his future welfare.

•—◆—•

He who marries for money,
his children shall be a curse to him.

•—◆—•

Only when the father tempts the son to commit sin
is disobedience justifiable.

Rabbi Meir said: "When the Israelites came to receive the Torah, God said to them: Bring Me good sureties that you will observe it." They answered: "Our Fathers will be our sureties." God answered: "Your sureties need sureties themselves. I have found fault with them." They answered our Prophets will be our sureties," God replied: "I have found fault with them also." Then the Israelites said. "Our children will be our sureties." They proved acceptable and God gave to Israel the Torah.

CHILDREN'S OBLIGATIONS

Where the children honor their parents,
there God dwells, there He is honored.

• ◆ •

The honor and reverence due to parents
are equal to the honor and reverence due to God.

• ◆ •

"Respect your parents as you respect Me," says God.

• ◆ •

A son must, if necessary, feed and support his parents.

• ◆ •

He who honors his father and mother enjoys the fruit
in this life, and stores up a treasure for the future.

While the son honors his parents,
God holds it as if He were dwelling near the child,
and were Himself receiving honor.

• ➤ •

Even if it happens that the son is a teacher, yet if the
father is present, the son must rise before him in the
presence of all his pupils.

• ➤ •

When a son is called to do a service for his parents,
he must first see that his person is tidy and clean;
for a child must attend to his parents
as though they were his king and queen.

• ➤ •

A child must not stand or sit in the place
which his father is in the habit of occupying.
He must not contradict his father,
and when he names him he must use
a term of respect, such as "my honored father."

• ➤ •

A child must love and honor his parents
while they are living, and must love and respect them
after they are dead; and as they loved and
honored God, he must love and honor God,
and thus make his parents live again
in his own good deeds.

If in after life the son prospers and is richer
than his father, he must see that his prosperity is shared
by his parents. He must not live in greater luxury than
they; he must not allow them to suffer poverty
while he enjoys wealth. But the son must not make
himself obnoxious by too many attentions.

Dama bar Netina, a heathen, of whom once some customers
desired to buy wheat, for which they offered him a high price
on account of its scarcity, said to them: "I cannot sell at
present, for the key to the store lies under the pillow whereupon my father is now asleep. I dare not disturb his rest."

LEANLINESS

Poverty comes from God, but not dirt.

LOTHING

In the town where one lives the name will do;
outside of it the dress must do.

The learned man whose garment is soiled
is undeserving of honor.

COMPASSION FOR ANIMALS

To have compassion upon animals
is one of the laws of Moses.

•—◆—•

He who has no mercy upon animals
shall himself suffer pain.

•—◆—•

Do not put a greater burden upon thy beast
than it can bear.

•—◆—•

People say: The burdens must be according to the camel.

•—◆—•

A man should not buy cattle or poultry
without having first bought food for them.

COMPLAINT

He who complains at his chastisements
receives a double portion of them.

•—◆—•

Keep far from complaint lest thou cause harm
to the innocent.

CONDUCT AND MANNERS

He who ponders upon his conduct
brings much good to himself.

• ◆ •

Be in the habit of receiving every man
with a pleasant countenance.

• ◆ •

Be humble to thy superior, affable to thy inferior,
meet every man with friendliness.

• ◆ •

The wiser the man, the more careful should he be
of his conduct.

• ◆ •

Thou hast entered the city; abide by its customs.

• ◆ •

Hillel said: Among those who stand, do not sit;
and among those who sit, do not stand.
Among those who laugh, do not weep;
and among those who weep, do not laugh.

• ◆ •

Great is etiquette! It is equal to the whole Torah.

ONFESSION

If a man confesses his sins before his Maker,
what labor does he leave to Satan?
Then Satan can do nothing but depart.

He who confesses has a share in the World-to-Come.

If a man confesses his guilt in a mortal court, he is
punished; if he does not admit it, he is sometimes freed.
In the Heavenly Court, however, it is the opposite:
if he confesses, he is forgiven; if he fails to confess,
he is doomed to punishment.

ONSEQUENCES

Into the well from which thou drinkest do not cast a stone.

ONSISTENCY

Beautiful are the admonitions of those whose lives
accord with their teachings.

The learned man should judge himself according
to his own teaching, and not do anything
that he has forbidden others to do.

ONTENTMENT

Who is rich? He who is satisfied with his lot.

• ◆ •

He is rich who enjoys what he possesseth.

• ◆ •

Little is much, if the heart be but turned toward heaven.

• ◆ •

One bird tied is better than a hundred flying.

• ◆ •

Drink not from one cup with thine eye fastened on another.

• ◆ •

A small quantity in the house is better than much
at a distance.

• ◆ •

Better eat onions all thy life than dine upon geese and
chickens once and then long in vain for more ever after.

• ◆ •

The egg of today is better than the hen of tomorrow.

OSMETICS

Cold water, morning and evening,
is better than all the cosmetics.

OVETOUSNESS

The eye sees and the heart covets.

．—◆—．

He who has a hundred desires two hundred.

．—◆—．

The question is asked, "Why is man born with
hands clinched, but has his hands wide open in death?"
And the answer is: On entering the world man desires
to grasp everything, but when leaving it
he takes nothing away.

．—◆—．

Many a man loves his riches
more than his soul.

．—◆—．

The camel wanted to have horns,
and they took away his ears.

$\mathcal{E}$ven as a fox who saw a fine vineyard,
and lusted after its grapes, but being too fat to
get through the only opening there was,
he fasted three days. He then got in; but, having fed,
he could not get out until he had fasted three days more.

•—◆—•

$\mathcal{C}$rave not after the table of kings: for thy table is greater
than their table, and thy crown is greater than their crown;
and the Master who employs thee is faithful
to pay the reward of thy labor.

•—◆—•

$\mathcal{G}$rasp a little and you may secure it;
grasp too much and you will lose everything.

•—◆—•

$\mathcal{H}$e that hires one garden will eat birds;
he that hires many gardens, the birds will eat him.

•—◆—•

$\mathcal{T}$he longest life is insufficient for the fulfillment
of half of man's desires.

EATH

$\mathcal{A}$ man does not tell lies in the hour of death.

A man cannot say to the Angel of Death,
I wish to arrange my affairs.

• ◆ •

Death is the haven of life,
and old age the ship which enters the port.

• ◆ •

It is our duty to comply with the last wishes
of a dying person.

 IGNITY

Dignity does not consist in a silk dress.

• ◆ •

It is unseemly for a lion to weep before a fox.

• ◆ •

No position can dignify the man. It is the man who
dignifies the position.

 ISCRETION

Thy friend has a friend,
and thy friend's friend has a friend; be discreet.

The mountains have eyes and the walls have ears.

• ◆ •

Keep shut the doors of thy mouth,
even from the wife of thy bosom.

• ◆ •

A man's merits should be fully stated in his absence,
but only partially in his presence.

• ◆ •

Teach thy tongue to say, "I do not know."

DUTY

As men are in duty bound to win the approval of God,
so are they in duty bound to win the approval
of their fellows.

DUTY TO GOD

Be bold as a leopard, light as an eagle, swift as a roe,
and strong as a lion, to do the will
of thy Father who is in heaven.

Hasten to the performance of the slightest
commandment, and flee from sin; for the
performance of one virtuous act leads to another,
and the commission of one sin leads to another;
so is the reward of one virtuous act the performance
of another, and the retribution of one sin
the commission of another.

• ◆ •

Regulate thy will in accordance with God's will, and
submit thy will to His will.

• ◆ •

What meaning "Thou shalt love the Lord thy God
with all thy soul"? It meaneth that thou must love Him,
even if He demand thy soul.

• ◆ •

Serve the Lord with joy, for the joy of man
draws towards him another joy from above.

• ◆ •

God's commandments are intended to enhance
the value and enjoyment of life,
but not to mar it and make it gloomy.

*I*t happened that a Judge of a city sent his servant to the market to purchase fish. When he reached the place of sale he found that all the fish but one had been sold, and this one a Jewish tailor was about purchasing. Said the Judge's servant: "I will give one gold piece for it;" said the tailor: "I will give two." Whereupon the other expressed his willingness to pay three gold pieces for it, but the tailor claimed the fish, and said he would not lose it though he were obliged to pay ten gold pieces for it. The Judge's servant then returned home, and in anger related the circumstance to his master. The judge sent for the tailor, and when the latter appeared before him he asked: "What is thy occupation?" "A tailor, sir," replied the man. "Then how canst thou afford to pay so great a price for a fish, and how dare you degrade my dignity by offering for it a greater sum than that offered by my servant?"

"I fast tomorrow," replied the tailor, "and I wished the fish to eat today, that I might have the strength to do so. I would not have lost it even for ten pieces of gold."

"What is tomorrow more than any other day?" asked the Judge.

"Why art thou more than any other man?" returned the other.

"Because the king has appointed me to this office."

"Well," replied the tailor, "the King of kings has appointed this day (the Day of Atonement) to be holier than all other days; on this day we hope that God will pardon our transgressions."

"If this be the case thou wert right," answered the Judge, and the Israelite departed in peace.

Thus if a person's intention is to obey God, nothing can hinder its accomplishment. On this day God commanded his children to fast, but they must strengthen their bodies to obey him by eating on the day before. It is a person's duty to sanctify himself, bodily and spiritually, for the approach of this great day.

•◆•

Six hundred injunctions, says the Talmud, was Moses instructed to give the people. David reduced them all to eleven in the fifteenth Psalm: Lord, who shall abide in Thy tabernacle, who shall dwell on Thy holy hill? He that walketh uprightly, and worketh righteousness, and speaketh the truth in his heart. He that backbiteth not with his tongue, nor doeth evil to his neighbor, nor taketh up with a reproach against his neighbor. In whose eyes a vile person is condemned; but he honoreth them that fear the Lord. He that sweareth to his own hurt, and changeth not. He that putteth not out his money to usury, nor taketh reward against the innocent. He that doeth these things shall never be moved.

The Prophet Isaiah reduced them to six: He that walketh righteously, and speaketh uprightly; he that despiseth the grain of oppressions, that shaketh his hands from holding of bribes, that stoppeth his ears from hearing of blood, and shutteth his eyes from seeing evil.

The Prophet Micah reduced them to three: What does the Lord require of thee but to do justly, and to love mercy, and to walk humbly with thy God?"

Isaiah once more reduced them to two: Keep ye judgment and do justice.

Amos reduced them all to one: Seek ye me and ye shall live.

EATING

Food is better for a man up to the age of forty;
after forty drink is better.

• ◆ •

The palate consumes the gold.

• ◆ •

Regard thy table as the table before the Lord.
Chew well, and hurry not.

• ◆ •

If words of the Torah are spoken at a meal,
it is as if God has shared in it.

ENVY AND JEALOUSY

Envy, lust, ambition, bring a man to perdition.

• ◆ •

An envious man frowns when his neighbor rejoices.

• ◆ •

He that cherishes jealousy in his heart,
his bones rot.

Bad neighbors count a man's income,
but not his expenses.

• ◆ •

The jealousy of scholars increases wisdom.

VIL

Evil thoughts are more deadly than sin itself.

• ◆ •

An evil eye, an "evil imagination," and misanthropy
banish a man from the world.

• ◆ •

Do not do good to the evil man,
and thou will not be repaid by evil.

• ◆ •

The "Spirit of Evil" entices a man in this world,
and testifies against him in the next.

• ◆ •

The "evil imagination" takes advantage
only of visible objects.

There is no greater evildoer than he
who takes away the earnings of the poor.

• ◆ •

God created the Evil Impulse,
but also the Torah as its antidote.

XPERIENCE

Experience is the mirror of the mind.

AME

He who seeks fame often loses it.

FAULTFINDING
AND BLAME

Man sees all the faults but his own.

• ◆ •

Do not blame in others your own faults.

Do not blame thy friend for shortcomings
which thou hast thyself.

• ◆ •

If any blame be attached to thee, be the first to declare it.

• ◆ •

First correct thyself, then correct others.

• ◆ •

He who seeks for a faultless brother
will have to remain brotherless.

• ◆ •

He who sees his own faults is too much occupied
to see the faults of others.

• ◆ •

He who blames others is full of blame himself;
and the fault he sees in others may be seen in himself.

• ◆ •

He who denies his guilt doubles his guilt.

EAR

The man bitten by a snake is afraid of a rope.

Why does a man have fear? Because his sins break his
courage and he has no strength left.

FLATTERY

Love those who reprove thee, and hate those who flatter
thee; for reproof may lead thee to eternal life,
flattery to destruction.

• ◆ •

A man may flatter his wife for the sake of marital peace;
his creditor for the sake of obtaining a respite; and his
teacher for the sake of obtaining more attention.

FLEXIBILITY

Man, be ever soft and pliable like a reed,
and not hard and unbending like a cedar.

FOOLS

There is no remedy for a fool.

Beware of an over-pious ignoramus
and of one badly trained.

• ◆ •

The fool thinks everyone else is a fool.

• ◆ •

Ignorance and conceit go hand in hand.

• ◆ •

The only thing to do with an idiot and a thorn
is get rid of them.

• ◆ •

A thing to which a fool does not consent,
know as the right thing.

• ◆ •

Rather be thou called a fool all thy days than walk
one hour before the All-Seeing Eye in evil ways.

• ◆ •

What is the sign of a foolish man?
He talks too much.

• ◆ •

For the blind in mind there is no physician.

• ◆ •

Do not live near a pious fool.

ORGIVENESS

He who wishes to be forgiven must forgive.

⋅◆⋅

It is sinful to hate, but noble to pardon.

⋅◆⋅

To accept excuse shows a good disposition.

FREE WILL

Everything is ordained by God's providence,
but freedom of choice is given to man.

⋅◆⋅

Say not that sin and crime come from God or that
He has caused thee to fall into sin, for He takes
no pleasure in a sinful man. He hates every wickedness
and abomination. He has created man from the beginning
in purity and has left him to his free will to follow
the path of righteousness or that of evil.

⋅◆⋅

Whether a man be strong or weak, rich or poor, wise or
foolish, depends mostly on circumstances that surround
him from the time of his birth, but whether a man be good
or bad, righteous or wicked, depends on his own free will.

RIENDSHIP

*F*riendship or death.

* ◆ *

*A*n old friend do not forsake.

* ◆ *

*A*scend a step in choosing a friend.

* ◆ *

*T*o have no faithful friends is worse than death.

* ◆ *

*I*f thy friend is honey, do not lick him up altogether.

* ◆ *

*G*et thee a companion,
one to whom you can tell your secrets.

* ◆ *

*O*ne enemy is one too many,
a thousands friends are none too many.

* ◆ *

*N*ew things are the best things;
old friends are the best friends.

* ◆ *

*H*e who asks more of a friend than he can bestow,
deserves to be refused.

At the gate of abundance there are many
brothers and friends; at the gate of misery
there is neither brother nor friend.

• ◆ •

Who is the greatest hero?
He who turns his enemy into a friend.

 GOD IN LIFE

The consciousness of God's presence
is the first principle of religion.

• ◆ •

Know that thou art always in God's Presence.

• ◆ •

From beginning to end God's law teaches kindness.

• ◆ •

Reverence of God is the basis of morality.

• ◆ •

Whatever God does is done for our good.

• ◆ •

How many miracles does God perform for man
of which man does not know?

There are three who are especially beloved by God; he who is forbearing, he who is temperate, and he who is courteous.

• ◆ •

Men should thank God alike for evil and for good.

• ◆ •

"If your God hates idolatry, why does He not destroy it?" Rufus, the Roman, asked Rabbi Akiba. "Would you have Him destroy this beautiful world for the sake of the foolish people who worship the sun, the moon, or the stars, that are but the servants of God?" Akiba replied.

GOOD NEIGHBORS

"Thou shalt love thy neighbor as thyself."
This is the greatest general rule in the Torah.

• ◆ •

Whatever is hateful to thee, do not to thy neighbor.

• ◆ •

Thy neighbor's property must be as sacred to thee
as thine own.

• ◆ •

Be as eager to secure thy fellow's honor as thine own,
and yield not easily to anger.

Guard with jealous care thy neighbor's honor.

• ◆ •

Hold your neighbor's honor as sacred as your own.

GOVERNMENT

Let the fear of government be always upon thee.

• ◆ •

A man must respect the government.

• ◆ •

He who revolts against the government
commits as great a sin as if he revolted against God.

• ◆ •

It is sinful to deceive the government
regarding taxes and duties.

• ◆ •

Pray for the welfare of the government,
since if it were not for the awe which it inspires,
men would swallow each other alive.

• ◆ •

Three things take in profusion and give in profusion;
the sea, the earth, and the government.

GREATNESS

Whosoever runs after greatness, greatness runs
away from him; he who runs from greatness,
greatness follows him.

How may a man obtain greatness?
By fidelity, truth, and lofty thoughts.

HABIT

Habit strips sin of its enormity.

Habit becomes natural.

THE HOME

A man rejoices when he dwells in his own home.

Every man is a king in his own home.

A home where Torah is not heard will not endure.

ONESTY

On the soul's appearance before the Divine Tribunal,
the first question will be, "Hast thou been honest
and faithful in all thy dealings?"

Always be sincere in your yea and your nay.

ONOR

Honor departs when it is sought
by the undeserving.

"Wherewith prolongest thou life?"
Rabbi Nechuma's disciples asked him once.
And the master answered:
"I never sought my honor at the expense
of my associate's degradation,
and the thought of a wrong done to me in daytime
never went with me to bed at night."

HOPE

Where there is life there is hope.

HOSPITALITY

Hospitality is as important as divine worship.

• ◆ •

Hospitality is greater than a visit to the House of Study;
it is greater than welcoming the Shekinah.
The hospitable man is rewarded in both worlds.

• ◆ •

Insist not that a man eat with thee if he does not desire it.

• ◆ •

Let thy house be open wide as a refuge,
and let the poor be cordially received within thy walls.

• ◆ •

The woman recognizes the worth of a guest
more than the man.

• ◆ •

Who is a despicable guest? One who brings along
another guest, and one who creates unusual bother.

HUMAN NATURE

Man is generally led the way which he is inclined to go.

• ◆ •

When one dog barks, he soon finds other dogs
to bark with him.

• ◆ •

Birds of a feather flock together; and so with men—
like to like.

HYPOCRISY AND DECEIT

Hypocrisy is like a woman who is in the apartment
of her lover, and swears by the life of her husband.

• ◆ •

Be not the friend of one who wears the cloak of a saint
to cover the moral deformities of a knave.

• ◆ •

Four classes of men will never see God's face—
the scoffer, the liar, the slanderer, the hypocrite.

• ◆ •

God hates the man who says one thing with his mouth
and another with his mind.

When the wicked are in trouble, they are submissive; but when their trouble is ended, they return to their evil ways.

• ◆ •

A lie has not a leg to stand upon.

• ◆ •

He who deceives his neighbor
would also deceive his God.

• ◆ •

He who pretends to be halt or blind in order
to appeal to popular sympathy, will be afflicted
with these infirmities sooner or later.

• ◆ •

The less the merits of a person are, the more
he will feel urged to proclaim them to the public.

• ◆ •

There are some who preach beautifully,
but practice not their beautiful doctrine.

• ◆ •

The pious fool, the hypocrite, and the flagellating
Pharisee are destroyers of human society.

• ◆ •

There are many persons who eat and drink together, yet
they pierce each other with the sword of their tongues.

A man can conceal himself from his enemies
but not from his friends.

•—◆—•

That which man conceals in his innermost chamber is
plain and manifest to God.

•—◆—•

*L*et not your lips speak that which is not in your heart.

•—◆—•

*A*n Israelite is prohibited from deceiving even an idolater.

IDLENESS

A man can quickly die if he has nothing to do.

•—◆—•

*W*hen the woman slumbers,
the work basket falls to the ground.

MMORTALITY AND
THE WORLD TO COME

*O*ne man may earn immortality by the work of a few short
years, while others earn it by the work of a long life.

$\mathcal{D}$o not speak ill of the departed, but remember that
his soul still lives, though the body is dead.

•—◆—•

$\mathcal{A}$ special mansion will be given in Heaven to every pious man.

•—◆—•

$\mathcal{B}$etter one hour's happiness in the next world than a
whole lifetime of pleasure in this.

•—◆—•

$\mathcal{H}$e who lays up no store of good deeds during the working
days of life can never enjoy the eternal Sabbath.

•—◆—•

$\mathcal{T}$he just of all nations have a portion in the future reward.

•—◆—•

$\mathcal{T}$his world is like a roadside inn,
but the world to come is like the real home.

•—◆—•

$\mathcal{T}$his world is an antechamber to the next.
Prepare thyself in the antechamber that thou mayest
worthily enter the throne-room.

•—◆—•

$\mathcal{T}$he grave is like a Melotian (silken) raiment for the pious
man, who comes fully provided with provisions;
the pious man can look upon the future life without fear,
because he comes to the other world well prepared.

"*M*an is born to die, but the dead shall live again."
"Better is the day of death than the day of birth."
These sayings are illustrated as follows: Two vessels sail
on the ocean at one and the same time; the one is leaving,
the other entering the harbor. For the one which arrived
a number of friends had prepared a great feast, and with
clapping of hands and great vociferations of joy, they
celebrated her arrival, while the one which was leaving
received sighs and tears. An intelligent man, who was a
spectator of what passed, said: "Here quite the reverse
appears to take place, as otherwise ought to happen. They
rejoice over the one which cometh and feel saddened over
the departure of the other. What a fallacy. Rejoice over the
one which has accomplished its voyage and is returning
from many dangers to safety, and bewail rather the vessel
which is coming in, for she will have to brave again the
storms of an inconstant sea." The same when man is born,
great rejoicing takes place, while at his death much grief is
expressed. One ought to weep at his birth, because no one
is certain whether he will be able to overcome the dangers
and temptations of life; whilst at his death one ought to
feel pleased if he only leaves a good name behind him.
At his birth man is entered into the book of death;
when he dies he is entered into the book of life.

• ◆ •

The shepherd is lame and the goats are nimble,
but at the entrance of the fold they will have to meet him
and at the door of the stable they will be counted.

UNGRATITUDE

When he was a puppy I fed him,
and when he became a dog he bit me.

• ◆ •

Despise not small favors.

• ◆ •

He who eats and drinks, but blesses not the Lord,
is even as he who stealeth.

• ◆ •

Once a man journeyed from Palestine to Babylon. While
at his meal, he noticed a fierce strife between two birds,
which ended in the apparent death of the one. When the
other, however, noticed that its companion was dead, it
hastened to search for a special kind of herb, which it
brought and laid on the beak of the corpse, and soon
thereafter the dead bird revived. The traveler saw this
with astonishment and procured a sample of the herb.
On journeying further, he met with a dead lion, and
concluded to make the experiment upon him. He
succeeded in reviving the lion, but no sooner had the
latter regained his strength than he tore his benefactor
to pieces.

SRAEL

*A*s it is impossible for the world to be without air,
so also is it impossible for the world to be without Israel.

●◆●

*E*verything depends on luck except Israel.

●◆●

*H*e who defends Israel is uplifted by God.

●◆●

*E*very nation has its special guardian angel, its horoscopes,
its ruling planets and stars. But there is no planet
for Israel. Israel shall look but to God.
There is no mediator between those who are called
His children and their Father which is in Heaven.

●◆●

*G*od loveth him who loveth Israel.

●◆●

*W*hy is Israel like an olive? As the olive gives its oil
only by being crushed, so does Israel repent
only through chastisements.

●◆●

*O*ne empire cometh and another passeth away,
but Israel abideth forever.

A king married a woman and made her magnificent
promises. Soon after he was obliged to leave her and
undertake a protracted journey. He stayed away a long
time, and the neglected wife was repeatedly offended
by her neighbors, who said: "The king has left thee; he
will never return." The poor woman wept and lamented,
but always regained comfort in the expectation of the
fulfillment of her husband's magnificent promises.
After a long time the king at last returned, and exclaimed:
"My beloved wife, I am really astonished at thy faithful
perseverance during so many years." "My lord and king,"
she rejoined, "if thy promises had not sustained me, I
had long ago succumbed to the advice of my neighbors."
This woman, such is the beautiful application, represents
Israel, who, in spite of all temptations and enticements
made by any other nations, faithfully bears the long
separation from God, hoping for the fulfillment of
the glorious promises contained in Holy Scriptures.

•—◆—•

*W*e read that while in the contest with Amalek,
Moses lifted up his arms, Israel prevailed.
Did Moses' hands make war or break war?
But this is to tell you that as long as Israel
is looking upward and humbling his heart
before his Father which is in heaven,
he prevails; if not, he falls.

OY

There is no joy like the joy of the heart.

• ◆ •

He who rejoices today
may not have cause for merriment tomorrow.
He who is troubled of heart today
may have no cause for anxiety tomorrow.
Joy does not await the pleasure of man.

UDGMENT

Judgment delayed is judgment voided.

• ◆ •

God alone can judge.

• ◆ •

In the hour when the Judge sits in judgment
over his fellow men, he shall feel, as it were,
a sword pointed at his own heart.

• ◆ •

Judge a man not according to the words of his mother,
but according to the comments of his neighbors.

Judge charitably every man and justify him all you can.

• ◆ •

Judge not thy neighbor until thou hast been placed
in his position.

• ◆ •

A certain man who was once hired to work for a stipulated
daily wage, and who worked for three years without having
drawn his earnings, at length desired to go home and
demanded his accumulations from his employer. "I have no
money just now," said the employer. "Give me then some
of your produce," demanded the employee. "I regret very
much," said the master, "that I cannot comply with thy
request." He asked him for cattle, for wine or vineyard, but
the master declared he was unable to give him anything.
With a heavy sigh the poor laborer took his tools and
without a murmur departed. Scarcely had he gone when the
employer ordered three asses laden with eatables, drinkables
and wearing apparel, and personally rode to the residence of
the laborer, who at once prepared a meal for his master, and
they ate and drank together. After a while the employer
drew forth a bag of money and handing it to the astonished
employee, told him that the provisions-laden asses were his
also. Thereupon the following dialogue ensued:

    EMPLOYER. "What was in thy mind when I told thee I
          had no money?"

    EMPLOYEE. "I thought thou hadst unfortunately lost it."

    EMPLOYER. "And when I told thee I had no cattle?"

EMPLOYEE. "That others claimed it for a debt incurred prior to mine."

EMPLOYER. "What couldst thou have thought when I told thee I had no field?"

EMPLOYEE. "That it might have been mortgaged."

EMPLOYER. "And when I told thee I had no fruit?"

EMPLOYEE. "That it might not have been tithed yet."

EMPLOYER. "But what didst thou think when I told thee I had no vineyard nor wine?"

EMPLOYEE. "It came to my mind that, perchance, thou hadst sanctified both wine and vineyard as gifts to the Temple."

EMPLOYER. "Ah, thou art a godly man. Faithfully hast thou complied with the ethical doctrine 'Judge everybody favorably.' Thou hast judged me favorably and God judge thee favorably."

JUSTICE

There is no true justice unless mercy is part of it.

The world is well conducted by two spinning wheels: one that spins justice, and the other than spins mercy.

When do justice and good will meet? When the contending parties are made to agree peaceably.

ABOR

Great is the dignity of labor; it honors man.

• ◆ •

A man should pray for the welfare of him
who gives him employment.

• ◆ •

Beautiful is the intellectual occupation,
if combined with some practical work.

• ◆ •

Get your living by skinning carcasses in the street,
if you cannot otherwise, and do not say,
"I am a priest, I am a great man;
this work would not befit my dignity."

• ◆ •

Love labor, shun office,
and do not cultivate intimacy with the authorities.

• ◆ •

He who helps himself will be helped by God.

• ◆ •

He who teaches his son no trade
is as if he taught him to steal.

He who does not teach his son a handicraft trade
neglects his parental duty.

• ◆ •

He who lives by the work of his hands is greater than
he who indulges in idle piety.

• ◆ •

He who derives his livelihood from the labor of his hands
is as great as he who fears God.

• ◆ •

Happy the child who sees its parents engage in
an honest trade; woe to the child who must blush
on account of their dishonest trade.

• ◆ •

It is well to add a trade to your studies;
you will then be free from sin.

• ◆ •

The laborer is allowed to shorten his prayers.

• ◆ •

The laborer at his work need not rise
before the greatest doctor.

• ◆ •

Work is more pleasant in the sight of the Lord
than the merits of your fathers.

HE LAW

The beginning and end of the Law is kindness.

• ◆ •

The study of the Law, when not sustained by secular work,
must come to an end, and involve one in sin.

• ◆ •

He who studies the Law in his youth gets its words
absorbed in his blood, and they come readily
from his mouth.

• ◆ •

He who studies the Law in his youth is like a
young man marrying a virgin, suited to him;
but he who begins the study of the Law in his old age
is like an old man marrying a virgin who suits him,
but who does not suit her.

LAWS OF NATURE

There is no rectangular thing in creation.

• ◆ •

The natural laws of the Universe do not change.

LEADERSHIP

The acts of the leader are the acts of the nation. If the leader is just, the nation is just; if he is unjust, the nation too is unjust and is punished for the sins of the leader.

•—◆—•

Too many captains sink the ship.

•—◆—•

Under no consideration lead men astray.

•—◆—•

Like generation, like leader.

•—◆—•

The serpent's tail had a long time followed the directions of the head with the best results. One day the tail began, "Thou appearest always foremost, but I must remain in the background. Why should I not also sometimes lead?" "Well," replied the head, "thou shalt have thy will for once." The tail, rejoiced, accordingly took the lead. Its first exploit was to drag the body into a miry ditch. Hardly escaped from that unpleasant situation, it crept into a fiery furnace; and when relieved from there, it got entangled among briers and thorns. What caused all these misfortunes? Because the head submitted to be guided by the tail. When the lower classes are guided by the higher, all goes well, but if the higher orders suffer themselves to be swayed by popular prejudices, they all suffer together.

LEARNING AND KNOWLEDGE

Had the Torah not been given, man could have
learned from the ant not to rob; from the dove not
to commit adultery; from the cat to be modest;
from the rooster to have good manners.

• ◆ •

A man cannot understand the Torah
unless he has stumbled in it.

• ◆ •

A man who has gold, but no knowledge—what has he?

• ◆ •

In the generation of Rabban Gamaliel,
do according to the opinions of Rabban Gamaliel;
in the generation of Rabbi Jose,
do according to the opinions of Rabbi Jose.

• ◆ •

The day on which the Torah was translated into Greek
was a mournful day unto Israel. It was like unto the day
when the Golden Calf was made. Why? Because the
Torah cannot be translated exactly like it ought to be.

• ◆ •

The upper waters are the Torah of the Scripture;
the lower waters are the Torah of Tradition.

"Wealth and riches are in his house,
and his benevolence standeth forever."
This describes the man who writes excellent books
and makes them easily available to others.

• ◆ •

A town which has no school should be abolished.

• ◆ •

The teachers are the guardians of a State.

• ◆ •

"Repeat," "repeat," that is the best medicine
for memory.

• ◆ •

He who instructs a child is as if he had created it.

• ◆ •

Honor the sons of the poor;
it is they who bring science into splendor.

• ◆ •

If you interrupt your studies for one day,
it will take you two to regain what you have lost.

• ◆ •

Jerusalem was destroyed because the instruction
of the young was neglected.

Teach the children of the poor without compensation,
and do not favor the children of the rich.

• ◆ •

The rivalry of scholars advances learning.

• ◆ •

To what may he be compared who teaches a child?
To one who writes on clean paper.

• ◆ •

He who acquires knowledge, without imparting it
to others, is like a myrtle in the desert,
where there is no one to enjoy it.

• ◆ •

Who are you whose prayers alone have prevailed?
I am a teacher of little children.

• ◆ •

You should revere the teacher even more than the father.
The latter only brought you into the world, the former
indicates the way into the next. But blessed is the son
who has learned from his father; he shall revere him
both as his father and his master; and blessed is
the father who has instructed his son.

• ◆ •

Learning becomes part of the very blood of him
who learns in his youth.

LEVITY

Beware of too much laughter,
for it deadens the mind and produces oblivion.

• ◆ •

Laughter and levity habituate a man to lewdness.

LIFE

Life is a passing shadow, says the Scripture.
Is it the shadow of a tower or a tree?
A shadow that prevails for a while?
No; it is the shadow of a bird in his flight—
away flies the bird and there is neither bird
nor shadow.

• ◆ •

Man is like that vegetation which sprouts from
the ground as a tender plant, and gradually grows
until at last it withers away and perisheth.
This, O man, should teach thee to live pleasurably,
enjoying the wealth that is thine while thou livest;
for, consider, how long may that be?
Life is brief, and death is sure.

OVE

*L*ove is blind to defects.

· ◆ ·

*L*ove inspired by unworthy motives dies
when those motives disappear.

· ◆ ·

*L*ove takes no advice.

· ◆ ·

*T*here is a compensation for everything
except our first love.

· ◆ ·

*H*e who loves thee scolds thee.

· ◆ ·

*T*he love which shirks from reproving is no love.

· ◆ ·

*L*ove without admonition is not love.

· ◆ ·

*T*hree things to produce love: culture of mind,
modesty, and meekness.

When our conjugal love was strong,
the width of the threshold offered sufficient
accommodation for both of us;
but now that it has cooled down,
a couch sixty yards wide is too narrow.

•◆•

A man fell in love with a woman who resided
in the block of the tanners. If she had not lived there,
he would never have entered this evil smelling section;
but, since she dwells there, the street seems to him
like the street of the perfumers.

MARRIAGE

God creates new worlds constantly. In what way?
By causing marriages to take place.

•◆•

Mating is as hard as cleaving the waters of the Red Sea.

•◆•

When a soul is sent down from Heaven, it is a combined
male and female soul. The male part enters the male child
and the female part enters the female. If they are worthy,
God causes them to re-unite in marriage.
This is true mating.

From the age of twenty, if a man remain in a state
of celibacy, he lives in constant transgression.
Up to that age the Holy One waits for him
to enter the state of matrimony,
and woe to his bones if he does not marry then!

• ◆ •

First build a house and plant a vineyard,
and then take a wife.

• ◆ •

From his first love man derives true wedded bliss.

• ◆ •

A man's home means his wife.

• ◆ •

Who is rich? He who has a good wife.

• ◆ •

An unkind wife is a mental affliction.

• ◆ •

Honor your wife that you may become rich.

• ◆ •

He who has no wife is esteemed as dead.

• ◆ •

Love your wife like yourself;
honor her more than yourself.

A true wife makes the home a holy place.

• ◆ •

As soon as a man marries his sins decrease.

• ◆ •

He who lives without a wife is no perfect man.

• ◆ •

A man should be careful not to afflict his wife,
for God counts her tears.

• ◆ •

Love your wife truly and faithfully,
and do not compel her to hard work.

• ◆ •

If thy wife is small, bend down to take her counsel.

• ◆ •

Let a man be careful to honor his wife,
for he owes to her alone all the blessings of his house.

• ◆ •

Let youth and old age not be joined in marriage,
lest the purity and peace of domestic life be disturbed.

• ◆ •

A man's wife has scarcely breathed her last
when another is waiting to take her place.

All the blessings of a household come through the wife, therefore should her husband honor her.

• ◆ •

All evils, but not an evil wife.

• ◆ •

It is as difficult to effect suitable matrimonial matches as it was to divide the Red Sea.

• ◆ •

To be unmarried is to live without joy, without blessing, without kindness, without religion, and without peace.

• ◆ •

A handsome dwelling, a pretty wife, and beautiful furniture, exert a cheering influence upon a man's spirits.

• ◆ •

He who loves his wife as his own self, and honors her more than himself, and he who educates his children in the right way, to him applies the Divine promise, "Thou shalt know that there is peace in thy tent."

• ◆ •

He who divorces his wife is hated before God.

• ◆ •

The majority of children resemble their maternal uncles; hence the choice of a wife should be determined by the character of her brothers.

When the wife of a man's youth dies,
the altar of the Lord is in mourning.

• ◆ •

He who sees his wife die before him has, as it were,
been present at the destruction of the Temple,
and around him the world grows dark.
It is woman alone through whom God's blessings
are vouchsafed to a house. She teaches the children,
speeds the husband to the house of worship and
instruction, welcomes him when he returns,
keeps the house godly and pure;
and God's blessings rest upon all these things.

MEDDLING

The meddler has his spoon in every pot.

MERCY

To deserve mercy, practice mercy.

• ◆ •

The mercy we to others show,
Heaven will show to us.

Whoever takes pity on his fellow beings,
on him God in heaven will take pity.

He who judges without mercy will himself be judged.

He who has compassion on his fellow man
is accounted of the true seed of Abraham.

Underneath the wings of the Seraphim
are stretched the arms of divine mercy,
ever ready to receive sinners.

ISERS

A miser is as wicked as an idolater.

The birds in the air even despise the miser.

The mice lie on his money bags.

There are persons who are chained to gold and silver.

Wealthy people are frequently miserly.

• ◆ •

Why are men like weasels?
A weasel gathers and knows not for what purpose.
So it is with men.

ODERATION

Be moderate in all things.

• ◆ •

Eat and drink to live; live not to eat and drink,
for thus do the beasts.

• ◆ •

More people die from overeating
than from undernourishment.

• ◆ •

Three things are good in a little measure
and evil in large: yeast, salt and hesitation.

• ◆ •

The horse fed too freely with oats oft becomes unruly.

• ◆ •

The sensible man drinks only when he is thirsty.

MODESTY AND HUMILITY

A good man is modest.

• ◆ •

Office seeks out the man who runs away from office.

• ◆ •

They who are modest will not easily sin.

• ◆ •

Who are the pious? The modest.
Who are the modest? Those who are bashful,
knowing that God sees them.

• ◆ •

He who humiliates himself will be lifted up;
he who raises himself up will be humiliated.

• ◆ •

God is the friend of the man who is humble.

• ◆ •

He who is humble in this world is distinguished
in the World-to-Come.

ONEY

*A*ttend no auctions if thou hast no money.

•—◆—•

*S*ilver purifies bastards.

•—◆—•

*W*ealth may be like waters gathered in a house,
which, finding no outlet, drown the owner.

•—◆—•

*T*he fortune of this world is like a wheel with two buckets,
the full becomes empty and the empty full.

•—◆—•

*H*e who loves money cannot be righteous,
and he who hastens after possessions
is led away from the right path.
Happy the rich whose hands are clean
and who do not cling to possessions.
If there be such a man,
we will praise him as happy,
for he has done much for his people.

•—◆—•

*P*eople say: Money is not found for important things,
but it is found for unimportant things.

OATHS

Do not accustom yourself to use oaths,
or you will be led into perjury.

❖

Swear not, even to the truth,
unless the court compels you to do so.

❖

The making of vows is the portal of folly.

❖

The world trembled with dread when God exclaimed:
"Take not my name in vain."

❖

Which is a vain oath? If one affirms impossibilities;
as, for instance, that a camel was flying in the air.

OBSCENITY

Let a man never allow an obscene word
to pass out of his mouth.

PINION

Despise not public opinion.

• ◆ •

The voice of the people is as the voice of God.

• ◆ •

He who fears the opinion of the world more than
his own conscience has but little self-respect.

• ◆ •

If one person tells thee that thou hast asses' ears,
do not mind it; but if two persons make this assertion,
at once place a pack-saddle upon thy back.

• ◆ •

If thy friends agree in calling thee an ass,
go and get a halter around thee.

PPORTUNITY

Opportunity falls into the hands of him
who is receptive towards it.

• ◆ •

While the fire is burning, slice your pumpkin and fry it.

PASSION

First, our passions are like travelers, making a brief stay,
then like guests visiting us day by day, until at last they
become our masters, holding us beneath their sway.

• ◆ •

*M*an's passions at first are like a cobweb's thread,
at last become like thickest cord.

• ◆ •

*T*he greater the man, the stronger his passion.

• ◆ •

*T*he wicked is in the power of his passion;
the righteous keeps passion in his power.

• ◆ •

*W*ere it not for the existence of passions,
no one would build a house, marry a wife,
beget children, or do any work.

• ◆ •

*W*hat should man do in order to live?
Deaden his passions. What should man do in order to die?
Give himself entirely to life.

• ◆ •

*W*ho is strong? He who subdues his passion.

PATRIOTISM AND COMMUNITY INVOLVEMENT

Do not isolate thyself from the community
and its interests.

• ◆ •

Those who work for the community shall work
without selfishness, but with the pure intention
to promote its welfare.

• ◆ •

Were it not for patriotism, sterile lands would be deserted.

PEACE

Peace is the name of God.

• ◆ •

The Bible was given to establish peace.

• ◆ •

Be a disciple of Aaron, loving peace, and pursuing peace.

• ◆ •

Blessings do not in the least avail
unless peace is included among them.

Be the first to hold out the hand of peace.

• ◆ •

What is sweeter than sweetness?
Peace after enmity.

• ◆ •

Where there is no peace, nothing flourishes.

• ◆ •

Sow peace at home, scatter its fruits abroad.

• ◆ •

Peace is equal to all else.

• ◆ •

Peace is the wisp of straw
which binds the sheaf of blessings.

• ◆ •

He who maketh peace among strivers
will inherit eternal life.

• ◆ •

Great is peace, for it is to the world
what yeast is to the dough.

• ◆ •

Peace is the vessel in which all God's blessings are
preserved to us and preserved by us.

Those who, when offended, do not give offence,
when hearing slighting remarks, do not retaliate,
they are the friends of God,
they shall shine forth like the sun in its glory.

• ◆ •

Have a soft reply to turn away anger,
and let thy peace be abundant with thy brother,
with thy friend, and with everybody,
even with the Gentile in the street,
that thou shalt be beloved above and esteemed below.

 ERJURY

The sin of perjury is great.

• ◆ •

God may delay all other punishments,
but the sin of perjury is avenged straightway.

 ERSECUTION

Be of them that are persecuted,
not of them that persecute.

Whosoever does not persecute them that persecute him,
whosoever takes an offence in silence,
he who does good because of love, he who is cheerful
under his sufferings—they are the friends of God.

• ◆ •

There is not a single bird more persecuted than the dove;
yet God has chosen her to be offered up on the altar.
The bull is hunted by the lion,
the sheep by the wolf, the goat by the tiger.
And God said: "Bring me a sacrifice, not from them
that persecute, but from them that are persecuted."

PHYSICIANS AND MEDICINE

A physician who takes no fee is worth no fee.

• ◆ •

God causes the remedial herbs to grow up from
the ground; they become a healing cause
in the hands of the physicians,
and from them the druggist prepares the remedies.

• ◆ •

If a physician cannot give his patient medicine
for his body, he should bring it about
that medicine be given him for his soul.

*A*cquire not the habit of drugs,
and avoid taking medicine if possible even when you are ill.

• ◆ •

*C*an a man live if he takes into his body nothing
but harmful drugs? If a man cannot fully combat
the habit of harmful drugs, at least let him
also take healthful ingredients.

• ◆ •

*M*edicine is a science whose practice is authorized
by God Himself.

• ◆ •

*T*he strict observance of Sabbath and the Day of
Atonement is set aside, when the physician declares such
desecration necessary, even against the will of the patient.

• ◆ •

*W*ait not to honor the physician till thou fallest sick.

• ◆ •

*W*e ought not to live in a town where no physician resides.

POVERTY

*H*ealthy poverty is opulence, compared with ailing wealth.

He who is poor in this world
will be rich in the World-to-Come.

The Eternal is the advocate of the poor.

The truly poor man is the unlearned man.

Neglect not thine own poor
in order to give to others who are poor.

Be mindful of the children of the poor,
for learning comes from them.

PRAYER

All are equal before God in prayer.

Always pray with humility and with a clear conscience.

Better little prayer with devotion
than much without devotion.

Blessed are the women who send their children
to the house of prayer.

•—◆—•

Cleanse your heart before praying.

•—◆—•

Even when the gates of heaven are shut to prayer,
they are open to those of tears.

•—◆—•

He who recites his prayer in a voice heard by others
is unworthy of trust.

•—◆—•

Look not on thy prayers as on a task;
let the supplication be sincere.

•—◆—•

Nothing can prevent prayer
from entering the Gate of Heaven.

•—◆—•

Only that man's prayer is answered who lifts his hands
with his heart in them.

•—◆—•

Prayer without devotion is like a body without life.
To pray loudly is not a necessity of devotion;
when we pray we must direct our hearts towards heaven.

$\mathcal{P}$ray and pray again. There will come an hour
when thy request will be granted.

• ◆ •

$\mathcal{P}$rayer is Israel's only weapon, a weapon inherited from
its fathers, a weapon tried in a thousand battles.

• ◆ •

$\mathcal{W}$hat is service in the heart? The answer comes "Prayer."

• ◆ •

$\mathcal{P}$rayer without concentration is like a body without a soul.

• ◆ •

$\mathcal{H}$e who prays with the community
will have his prayer granted.

PREPAREDNESS

$\mathcal{S}$pread out the snare for the wolf
before he comes to the flock.

PROMISES

$\mathcal{G}$ood men promise little and perform much.
Wicked men promise much and perform nothing.

QUARRELLING AND DISCORD

A quarrel is like a stream of water.
If it has once opened a way,
it becomes a wide path.

• ◆ •

No good results from a quarrel.

• ◆ •

Quarreling is the weapon of the weak.

• ◆ •

When food is lacking in the larder,
quarrel knocks at the door.

• ◆ •

When two men quarrel,
he who is first silent is the better man.

• ◆ •

Discord is like a leak in a cistern.
Drop by drop all the water escapes.

• ◆ •

Strife is like a jet of water pouring through a crevice;
the wider the crevice, the stronger the flow.

ELIGION

Religion is the light of the world.

• ◆ •

He who devotes himself to the mere study of religion
without engaging in works of love and mercy
is like one who has no God.

• ◆ •

Religion maketh the man.

• ◆ •

Without religion there can be no true morality.

• ◆ •

He who denies a child religious knowledge
robs him of his inheritance.

• ◆ •

He who disturbs the peace disturbs God,
whose Name is Peace.

EPENTANCE

Why is repentance likened to the sea?
As the sea is open at all times, so is the gate of penitence.

When can penitence atone for a man's sin?
If his conscience still troubles him regarding it.
If a man's conscience ceases to trouble him,
penitence will not avail.

• ◆ •

Happy the man who repents
in the strength of his manhood.

• ◆ •

Not sackcloth and fasting avail,
but repentance and good deeds.

• ◆ •

One contrition in man's heart
is better than many flagellations.

• ◆ •

The aim and end of all wisdom
are repentance and good works.

• ◆ •

As the ocean never freezes,
so the gates of repentance never close.

• ◆ •

So great is the virtue of repentance
that it prolongs a man's years.

The tears of true penitence are not shed in vain.

• ◆ •

He who repeatedly sins, looking forward to penitence to cover his sins, his penitence will avail him nothing.

• ◆ •

Even the most righteous shall not attain to so high a place in heaven as the truly repentant.

• ◆ •

Repentance in old age is of lesser value, since a man is not tempted to do evil as much as in the years of his youth.

• ◆ •

One hour employed in this world in the exercise of repentance and good deeds is preferable to a whole life in the world to come; and one hour's refreshment of spirit in the future world is preferable to the entire life in this.

• ◆ •

The Day of Atonement is given for the expiation of sins committed against God; but the Day of Atonement will not expiate sins committed against a fellow man, unless the offender has asked pardon of the offended.

• ◆ •

In three ways may we repent; by publicly confessing our sins, by manifesting sorrow for sins committed, and by good deeds, which are as sacrifices before the Lord.

God knew that man would be prone to sin,
and He therefore created Repentance before He made man.

• ◆ •

Repent one day before thy death. There was a king who
bade all his servants to a great repast, but did not indicate
the hour; some went home and put on their best garments
and stood at the door of the palace, others said, "There is
ample time, the king will let us know beforehand." But the
king summoned them of a sudden, and those that came in
the best garments were well received, but the foolish ones
who came in their slovenliness were turned away in disgrace.
Repent today lest tomorrow ye might be summoned.

• ◆ •

There is more joy in Heaven over one sinner who
repenteth than over ninety and nine righteous persons,
who need no repentance.

• ◆ •

An arrow carries the width of a field;
but repentance carries to the very throne of God.

REPROOF

He who cannot bear one word of reproof
will have to hear many.

RESIGNATION AND ACCEPTANCE

*B*lessed is he who meekly bears his trials,
of which everyone has his share.

• ◆ •

*D*uring Rabbi Meir's absence from home two of his sons
died. Their mother, hiding her grief, awaited the father's
return, and then said to him: "My husband, some time
since two jewels of inestimable value were placed with
me for safe keeping. He who left them with me called
for them today, and I delivered them into his hands."
"That is right," said the Rabbi, approvingly. "We must
always return cheerfully and faithfully all that is left in
our care." Shortly after this the Rabbi asked for his sons,
and the mother, taking him by the hand, led him gently
to the chamber of death. Meir gazed upon his sons, and
realizing the truth, wept bitterly. "Weep not, beloved
husband," said his noble wife; "didst thou not say to
me we must return cheerfully, when 'tis called for, all
that has been placed in our care? God gave us these
jewels, he left them with us for a time, and we gloried
in their possession; but now that he calls for his own,
we should not repine."

Rabbi Judah said: "If a person weeps and mourns
excessively for a lost relative, his grief
becomes a murmur against the will of God,
and he may soon be obliged to weep for another death.
We should justify the decree of God,
and exclaim with Job,
'The Lord gave and the Lord hath taken;
blessed be the name of the Lord.'"

When misfortune befalls you examine your conduct
and acknowledge that God's chastisement is just.

REVENGE

Misery and remorse are the children of revenge.

He who gratifies revenge destroys his own house.

He who returns evil for evil acts wrongly.

The spittle, which a man throws upward,
will fall upon his own face.

Rabbi Meir was vociferous against evildoers and often prayed God, saying, "Destroy the sinners." Beruriah, his pious wife, gently admonished him, saying, "Rather pray that God destroy sin and the sinners will be no more."

EWARDS

The reward of good works is like dates;
sweet and ripening late.

• ◆ •

Be not like servants who wait on their master
expecting to receive reward, but be you like those
who serve their master without expecting reward.

• ◆ •

God has confused the reward promised to those who
perform Mitzwot, so that they may perform them
as an act of loyalty to Him.

• ◆ •

In proportion to thy efforts will be thy recompense.

• ◆ •

The measure man metes to man
the same will be meted to him.

THE RIGHTEOUS

The righteous promise little and do much.

• ◆ •

Alexander one day wandered to the gates of paradise
and knocked. The guardian angel asked: "Who is there?"
"I, Alexander." "Who is Alexander?" "Alexander,
the conqueror of the world." "We know him not.
He cannot enter here. This is the Lord's gate;
only the righteous enter here."

• ◆ •

The righteous are even greater in death than in life.

• ◆ •

The righteous man is a pillar
upon which all the world rests.

• ◆ •

The righteous are heard when they persevere in prayer.

• ◆ •

The righteous need no monuments.
Their deeds are their monuments.

• ◆ •

The death of the righteous is a calamity
equal in magnitude to the burning of the Temple.

When the righteous die, they live; for their example lives.

• ◆ •

For the righteous there is no rest, neither in this world
nor in the next, for they go, say the Scriptures,
"from strength unto strength, from task to task,
until they shall see God in Zion."

THE SABBATH

What was created on the Sabbath day?
Contentment, peace of mind, and physical rest.

• ◆ •

What is the foretaste of the World-to-Come?
The Sabbath.

• ◆ •

He who observes properly one Sabbath is as if
he had observed every Sabbath since it was ordained.

• ◆ •

One Rabbi declared that the Sabbath was given for
delight, namely for a pleasant time. Another declared
that it was given for study. But there is no variance
between them. Those who study during the week
shall rest and enjoy the Sabbath. Those who do not
study during the week shall do so on the Sabbath.

The Sabbath is given to man,
not man to the Sabbath.

• ◆ •

He who takes delight in the Sabbath,
receives his heart's desires.

• ◆ •

The Sabbath is a Queen whose coming
changes the humblest home into a palace.

• ◆ •

Rabbi Aibo said: "Rest yourself on the Sabbath
from thinking mundane thoughts."

SECRETS

Thy secret is thy slave. If thou let it loose,
thou becomest its slave.

• ◆ •

Do not reveal thy secret to the apes.

• ◆ •

Though thousands do thy friendship seek,
To one alone thy secret speak.

SELF-RESPECT

Hillel said: "If I am not for myself, who will be,
but if I am only for myself, what am I?"

• ◆ •

He who is bashful before others but is not before himself
is wanting in self-respect.

SELF-SUFFICIENCY

A person dependent on the table of another
has the world darkened.

• ◆ •

A man should be opposed to taking alms
as well as to being a burden on the community.

• ◆ •

Whoever has no possessions may be compared
to an infant that has lost its mother. It may be
nourished by many women, but it does not thrive,
because a mother's love no one is able to supply.
The man who is supported by others, were it even by his
own father or mother, or his children, never feels that
contentment which his own exertions would give him.

*I*t is better to be a menial
than to live upon the charity of others.

SERMONS

*T*here is a time for long services and long sermons,
and a time for short ones.

*T*hou preachest beautifully, but is thy practice beautiful?

SHAME

*H*e who is ashamed will not easily commit sin.

*T*here is great difference between him
who is ashamed before his own self
and him who is only ashamed before others.

*T*here is hope for a man who is capable of being ashamed.

*H*e who transgresses and feels ashamed is forgiven.

ICKNESS AND PAIN

*E*very ache, but not a headache!

• ◆ •

*H*eartache is the most painful of aches.

• ◆ •

*H*e who visits the sick prolongs their life.

• ◆ •

*I*f your neighbor is sick, pray for him.

• ◆ •

*N*o man in the world is free from pain.

ILENCE

*S*ilence is as good as agreement.

• ◆ •

*I*f silence is becoming to a wise man,
how much more so to a fool?

• ◆ •

*F*or every evil, silence is the best remedy.

Rabbi Simeon said: "I have been brought up all my life among the wise and I have never found anything of more benefit to man than silence."

If a word spoken in time is worth one piece of money, silence in its time is certainly worth two.

SIN

Sin begets sin.

A transgression hardens the heart.

Curse the sin, not the sinner.

Commit a sin twice, and you will think it perfectly allowable.

Every sin of a man is engraved upon his bones.

No man sins for someone else.

To resist sin is as meritorious
as to be actively engaged in good work.

• ◆ •

Rabbi Johanan claimed that only a handbreath,
the width of four inches, separates Hell and Heaven.

• ◆ •

He who raises a hand against a fellow man,
even if he injure him not, is called wicked.

• ◆ •

He through whose agency another has been
falsely punished stands outside of heaven's gates.

• ◆ •

The righteous control their desires,
but the desires of the wicked control them.

• ◆ •

There is no death without individual sin,
no pain without individual transgression.

• ◆ •

That same spirit that dictated in the Pentateuch:
"And parents shall not die for their children,
nor the children for their parents,"
has ordained that no one should be punished
for another's transgressions.

• ◆ •

Sinful thoughts are even more dangerous than sin itself.

SLANDER AND GOSSIP

To slander is to murder.

• ◆ •

Better no ear at all than one that listeneth to evil.

• ◆ •

Guard thy mouth from uttering an unseemly word.

• ◆ •

Rather be thrown into a fiery furnace
than bring anyone to public shame.

• ◆ •

This is the way of gossipers:
They commence with praise and end with derogation.

• ◆ •

Oftentimes a man praises his fellow in a low voice
but derides him in a loud.

• ◆ •

A slanderer injures three persons: himself,
him that receives the slander and the slandered person.

Even if all the words of slander are not accepted as true,
half of them are accepted.

*L*isten, sir, to my words, and give ear to my utterances.
Keep from strifes with thy neighbor, and if thou
seest that thy friend does anything wrong,
guard thy tongue from gossip.

R. Gamaliel ordered his servant Tobi to bring something
good from the market, and he brought a tongue.
At another time he told him to bring something bad,
and he also returned with a tongue.
"Why did you on both occasions fetch a tongue?"
the Rabbi asked. "It is the source of good and evil,"
Tobi replied, "if it is good there is nothing better,
and if it is bad there is nothing worse."

*H*e who shames a fellow man in public is a murderer.

SOLDIERS

Soldiers fight and the kings are called heroes.

THE SOUL

The soul of one good man is worth as much as all the earth.

The soul consists of three parts:
power of life, power of endurance,
and the power of higher feeling.

• ◆ •

God is pure, and the soul He gave thee is pure.

• ◆ •

Hillel, the gentle, the beloved sage,
Expounding day by day the sacred page
To his disciples in the house of learning;
And day by day, when home at eve returning,
They lingered, clust'ring round him, loath to part
From him whose gentle rule won every heart.
But evermore, when they were wont to plead
For longer converse, forth he went with speed,
Saying each day: "I go—the hour is late—
To tend the guest who doth my coming wait,"
Until at last they said: "The Rabbi jests
When telling us thus of his daily guests
That wait for him." The Rabbi paused awhile,
Then made answer: "Think you I beguile
You with an idle tale? Not so forsooth!
I have a guest, whom I must tend in truth.
Is not the soul of a man indeed a guest,
Who in this body deigns awhile to rest,
And dwells with me all peacefully today;
Tomorrow—may it not have fled away?"

Such is the way of God: he giveth to all alike a precious gift, a pure and spotless soul. The pious who make good use of this divine gift are permitted to enjoy eternal bliss, but the wicked are debarred from this happiness, till their souls are purified from the taints of sin.

TEAMWORK

One loose cord loosens many.

TEMPERAMENT

There are four kinds of temperament:
To be easily provoked, and to be easily pacified,
is to neutralize a bad quality with a good one;
to be provoked with difficulty, and to be pacified with
difficulty, is to neutralize a good quality by a bad one;
to be provoked with difficulty, and to be easily pacified,
is the temperament of a holy man;
to be easily provoked and pacified with difficulty
is the temperament of a wicked man.

• ◆ •

One who restrains his temper,
all his sins meet forgiveness.

TEMPTATION

Happy the man who resists his temptations.

No man should lead himself into temptation.

Place no temptation in the path of the honest man;
and the same is all the more true for the dishonest.

The study of God's Word
is the only antidote against temptation.

THEFT

If the thief has no opportunity,
he thinks himself honorable.

Do not buy stolen goods.

He who unjustly hands over one man's goods to another,
he shall pay God for it with his own soul.

"What induces theft?" asked a schoolmaster of his scholars. One answered "Hunger"; another "Extravagance"; another "Envy." But one, wiser than the rest, replied "Receivers." "Well answered," said the schoolmaster. "For King Solomon says, 'Whoever is partner with a thief hateth his own soul,' which means, he who derives gain from a thief by helping him to realize the profit of the theft is thoroughly dishonest himself, and of the two is the more culpable."

• ◆ •

Buy nothing from a thief.

• ◆ •

If one finds a marked article he should advertise it publicly, so that the owner may recover it.

• ◆ •

It is wrong to receive a present from a thief.

• ◆ •

Neither the Day of Atonement nor even repentance will suffice to expiate the sin of robbery; full restitution must come first.

The thief's end is the gallows.

• ◆ •

The receiver is as bad as the thief.

There is no difference between robbing a Jew
or robbing a Gentile; if any, to rob a Gentile
is a greater sin than to rob a Jew.

THRIFT

Live within your means; spend more on your clothing
and most on your home.

⚫—◆—⚫

A penny added to a penny creates in the end a large sum.

TOLERANCE

"Before me," said the Lord, "there is no difference
between Jew and Gentile; he that accomplishes good,
will I reward accordingly."

⚫—◆—⚫

The virtuous of all nations participate in eternal bliss.

⚫—◆—⚫

Wrong neither thy brother in faith
nor him who differs from thee in faith.

When Abraham left Ur in Chaldea, he settled near Bethel, for the pasturage was good, the country well watered, with a very scanty population, at which he rejoiced, as his flocks could graze unmolested. But Sarah lamented their late pleasant home, on the plain, Moreb, and their friendly neighbors. Being tired of their solitude, she begged her husband to invite any wayfarers to their tent to partake of their hospitality. One day Abraham noticed an old man riding as one in haste, and, inquiring of him the cause, discovered the man to be in search of a scattered herd of cattle, so he invited him to his tent to refresh himself, promising that some of his young men would assist in the search. The old man assented. Abraham had a bath prepared and a goodly feast, prior to the eating of which Abraham invoked a blessing from God, in which the old man refused to join. On being asked the reason for his impiety he acknowledged being a fire worshipper. Abraham, full of indignation at his refusal to join in prayer, drove the travel-worn old man out of his tent. As he departed sorrowfully an angel of the Lord appeared to Abraham and asked him what he did, saying: "See you not that the Lord has had patience with this ignorant man these seventy years—can you not dwell with him for an hour?"

So Abraham recalled the old man, urged him to partake, made ready his young men, who soon returned with the missing cattle, and who assisted the traveller to drive them home; on which the old man, in leaving, blessed Abraham and Sarah, and said their kindly actions made a believer of him, and that a living fire was burning in his heart to be of service to his fellow man.

RIALS

Blessed be he who bears his trials.
Everyone has his share.

•—◆—•

Bodily sufferings purge away sin.

•—◆—•

He who cheerfully submits to sufferings
brings salvation to the world.

•—◆—•

The future gains from present pains.

•—◆—•

There is no tribulation which overtakes a man without
some benefit to others.

•—◆—•

Why is Israel likened unto an olive? Because as the olive
does not yield its oil until it is pressed, so the people of
Israel do not repent until they are afflicted.

RUTH

Truth is the seal of God.

Always acknowledge the truth.

• ◆ •

Everything has been created by God,
except falsehood.

• ◆ •

Truth is heavy; therefore few wear it.

• ◆ •

Truth is its own witness.

• ◆ •

Truth will stand, but falsehood must fall.

• ◆ •

Deception in words is a greater sin
than deception in money matters.

• ◆ •

To be faithless to a given promise
is as sinful as idolatry.

• ◆ •

This is the punishment of the liar,
that when he tells the truth nobody believes him.

• ◆ •

To break a verbal engagement,
though legally not binding, is a moral wrong.

USEFULNESS

*I*n all God's creation there is not a single object
without a purpose.

•◆•

*U*se thy best vase today,
for tomorrow it may, perchance, be broken.

VIRTUE

*W*hat is the prime virtue?
To be pure in the eyes of God and man.

•◆•

*T*he forest trees once asked the fruit trees:
"Why is the rustling of your leaves not heard
in the distance?" The fruit trees replied:
"We can dispense with the rustling to manifest
our presence, our fruits testify for us."
The fruit trees then inquired of the forest trees:
"Why do your leaves rustle almost continually?"
"We are forced to call the attention of man
to our existence."

INE

When wine enters, reason departs,
and secret thoughts are revealed.

◆

Drink not, and you will not sin.

◆

In a place where there is no wine,
drugs are needed.

◆

The good wine and the good waters have been the
misfortune of the Ten Tribes.

◆

Two things cannot go hand in hand;
drinking wine and serving the Lord prayerfully.

◆

When Satan cannot come himself,
he sends wine as a messenger.

◆

Where there is wine, there is no sense.

WISDOM

Wisdom is a tree and active virtue is its fruit.

· ◆ ·

A scholar is greater than a prophet.

· ◆ ·

Study is more meritorious than sacrifice.

· ◆ ·

Let thy house be a resort of the wise.

· ◆ ·

Who is a wise man? He who learns of all men.

· ◆ ·

Who is a wise man? He who looks into the future.

· ◆ ·

The end of wisdom is repentance and good works.

· ◆ ·

There is no Torah without wisdom,
and no wisdom without Torah; both are one.

· ◆ ·

Learn a little here and a little there,
and you will increase in knowledge.

If a man has knowledge, he has all things;
if he has no knowledge, he has nothing.

• ◆ •

Culture of heart is better than culture of learning.

• ◆ •

The chief thing is not learning, but the deed.

• ◆ •

If a man does not go after wisdom,
wisdom will not come to him.

• ◆ •

Whosoever tries to make gain
by the crown of learning perishes.

• ◆ •

The more knowledge, the more spiritual life.

• ◆ •

Wisdom increases with years; and so does folly.

• ◆ •

God looks to the heart of man and then to the mind.

• ◆ •

The Lord is not with him who,
while possessing great knowledge,
has no sense of duty.

If you have not desired wisdom in your youth,
how will you acquire her in your old age?

• ◆ •

Do not be wise in words alone, but also in deeds, for the
wisdom of deeds will be necessary for the world to come,
while the wisdom of words remains on earth.

• ◆ •

The ultimate end of all knowledge and wisdom
is man's inner purification and the
performance of good and noble deeds.

• ◆ •

Without knowledge there can be
neither true morality nor piety.

• ◆ •

Be eager to acquire knowledge;
it does not come to thee by inheritance.

• ◆ •

Cling steadfastly to that which is good.

• ◆ •

It is necessary to have a knowledge of the world,
besides a knowledge of the Holy Law.

• ◆ •

None may be called venerable save the wise.

Be wise, my son, be prescient, acquire truth and esteem uprightness. Look upon fools as empty shadows. Avoid the advice of the ignorant; build when he advises to tear down, and attach yourself to the wise.

·—◆—·

When the wise is angry, he is wise no longer.

Four dispositions are found among those who sit for instruction before the wise, and they may be respectively compared to a sponge, a funnel, a strainer, and a sieve; the sponge imbibes all; the funnel receives at one end and discharges at the other; the strainer suffers the wine to pass through, but retains the lees; and the sieve removes the bran, but retains the fine flour.

·—◆—·

People say: "In a discussion one decisive point is worth many indecisive ones."

WOMAN

A woman loves a poor youth rather than a rich old man.

·—◆—·

A woman schemes while plying the spindle.

There is no end to the goodness of a good woman,
nor is there any end to the wickedness of an evil woman.

• ◆ •

A woman is more desirous of entering
the state of matrimony than a man.

• ◆ •

A woman prefers poverty with the affection
of her husband to riches without it.

• ◆ •

A woman's weapons are always with her.

• ◆ •

A shrewish woman is like a disease of the skin.
Both are easiest to bear when they are not touched.

• ◆ •

An old man is a trouble in the house;
an old woman is a treasure in the house.

• ◆ •

Culture in a woman is better than gold.

• ◆ •

God has endowed women with a special sense of wisdom
which men lack.

The Emperor Hadrian is introduced as conversing with Rabbi Gamaliel on several religious questions, with the object of casting ridicule on the Bible. Hadrian exclaims: "Why, your God is represented therein as a thief. He surprised Adam in his sleep and robbed him of one of his ribs." The Rabbi's daughter, who is present, craves permission to reply to the Emperor. This is granted. "But first let me implore thy imperial protection, puissant sire," she exclaims. "A grave outrage has been perpetrated upon our house. Under the cover of night an audacious thief broke into our house and took a silver flagon from our chest of plate and left a golden one in its stead." "What a welcome thief," cried Hadrian. "Would that such robbers might visit my palace every day." "And was not the Creator such a thief as this?" archly rejoins the dashing damsel—"Who deprived Adam of a rib and in lieu thereof gave him a loving, lovely bride?"

WORDS

The value of the words uttered with the lips
is determined by the devotion of the heart.

Speech is the messenger of the heart.

A word once spoken ascends to Heaven,
and prepares for the speaker good or evil
as his portion in the World-to-Come.

• ◆ •

Every word, whether good or bad,
accidental or intentional, is recorded in a book.

• ◆ •

He who utters blessings is blessed;
he who utters curses is cursed.

WORRY AND CARE

Do not worry thyself with the trouble of tomorrow;
perhaps thou wilt have no trouble tomorrow,
and why shouldst thou trouble thyself
about a world that is not thine?

• ◆ •

Let not your heart with cares be filled,
for care has many a victim killed.

• ◆ •

A sigh breaks half the body.

OUTH

Youth is a crown of roses,
old age is a crown of rosemary.

• ◆ •

Alas! for one thing that goes and never returns.
What is it? Youth.

• ◆ •

Happy is he who fears God
when in the prime of life.

• ◆ •

Happy is our youth if it leaves no memories in old age
of which we are ashamed.

• ◆ •

Some are old in their youth,
others young in their old age.

• ◆ •

If you do not bend the twig of a vine when it is young,
you cannot bend it when it hardens.

Index

℘

Pain. *See* Sickness and pain; Trials.

Palestine Talmud. *See* Jerusalem Talmud.

Pardon. *See* Forgiveness.

Parents
duty of, to children, 36–37
honoring of, by children, 38–40

Passion, 97

Patriarch, The. *See* Judah ha-Nasi.

Patriotism and community involvement, 98

Peace, 98–100

Penitence. *See* Repentance.

Pentateuch. *See* Torah.

Perjury, 95, 100

Persecution, 100–101

Physicians and medicine, 101–102, 133

Pious, the, 56, 57, 93

Pity. *See* Mercy.

Pliability. *See* Flexibility.

Poor, the. *See* Charity and good deeds; Poverty.

Pope Julius XII, 12–13

Pope Leo X, 12

Poverty, 40, 102–103

Prayer, 103–105

Preaching, 118

Preparedness, 105

Pride. *See* Arrogance and pride.

Prince, The. *See* Judah ha-Nasi.

Promises, 105, 114

Purification, as order of the Mishnah, 6

Q

Quarrelling and discord, 106

ℛ

Ramban. *See* Nahman, Moses ben.

Ran. *See* Reuben Gerondi, Nissim ben.

Rashba. *See* Adret, Solomon ben.

Rashi. *See* Yitzchaki, Sholomo.

Religion, 107

Repentance, 107–110. *See also* Confession.

Reproof, 110

Reputation. *See* Character and reputation.

Resignation and acceptance, 111–112

Reuben Gerondi, Nissim ben (Ran), 12

Revenge, 112–113

Rewards, 113

THE BUDDHA'S GOLDEN PATH
The Classic Introduction to Zen Buddhism
Dwight Goddard

In 1929, when author Dwight Goddard wrote *The Buddha's Golden Path,* he was breaking ground. No American before him had lived the lifestyle of a Zen Buddhist monk, and then set out to share the secrets he had learned with his countrymen. This title was the first American book published to popularize Zen Buddhism. Released in the midst of the Great Depression, in its own way, it offered answers to the questions that millions of disillusioned people were beginning to ask—questions about what was really important in their lives. Questions we still ask ourselves today.

As a book of instruction, *The Buddha's Golden Path* has held up remarkably well. As a true classic, it has touched countless lives, and has opened the door for future generations in this country to study and embrace the principles of Zen.

$14.95 • 208 pages • 5.5 x 8.5-inch quality paperback • 2-color • Religion/Zen Buddhism • ISBN 0-7570-0023-1

BUSHIDO
The Way of the Samurai
Tsunetomo Yamamoto • Translated by Minoru Tanaka
Edited by Justin F. Stone

In eighteenth-century Japan, Tsunetomo Yamamoto created the *Hagakure,* a document that recorded his thoughts on samurai values and conduct. For the next two hundred years, the *Hagakure* was secretly circulated among the "awakened" samurai—the samurai elite. In 1906, the book was first made available to the general Japanese public, and until 1945, its guiding principles greatly influenced the Japanese ruling class—particularly those individuals in military power. However, the spirit of the *Hagakure* touched a deeper nerve in Japanese society. It was this book that shaped the underlying character of the Japanese psyche, from businessmen to politicians, from students to soldiers.

Bushido: The Way of the Samurai is the first English translation of the *Hagakure.* From its opening line, "I have found the essence of Bushido: to die!" this work provides a powerful message aimed at the spirit, body, and mind of the samurai warrior. It offers beliefs that are difficult for the Western mind to embrace, yet fascinating in their pursuit of absolute service. By reading this book, one can better put into perspective the historical path that Japan has taken for the last three hundred years, and gain greater insight into the Japan of today.

$9.95 • 128 pages • 5.5 x 8.5-inch quality paperback • 2-color • Philosophy/Martial Arts • ISBN 0-7570-0026-6

TAO TE CHING
The Way of Virtue
Lao Tzu • Translated by Patrick Michael Byrne

The *Tao Te Ching* has served as a personal road map for millions of people. It is said that its words reveal the underlying principles that govern the world in which we live. Holding to the laws of nature—drawing from the essence of what all things are—it offers both a moral compass and an internal balance. A fundamental book of the Taoist, the *Tao Te Ching* is regarded as a revelation in its own right. For those seeking a better understanding of themselves, it provides a wealth of wisdom and insights.

Through time—from one powerful dynasty to another—many changes have been made to the original Chinese text of the *Tao Te Ching*. Over the last century, translators have added to the mix by incorporating their interpretations. While jackhammering its original text, some have created beautiful versions of the *Tao Te Ching* in the name of poetic license. Others have relied on variant forms of the original, while still others have added their own philosophical spins to the material. For those readers who are looking for a purer interpretation of the *Tao Te Ching*, researcher Patrick Michael Byrne has produced a translation that is extremely accurate, while capturing the pattern and harmony of the original. Here is a *Tao Te Ching* that you can enjoy, understand, and value.

$14.95 • 176 pages • 5.5 x 8.5-inch quality paperback • 2-color • Spiritualism/Chinese • ISBN 0-7570-0029-0

I CHING FOR A NEW AGE
The Book of Answers for Changing Times
Edited by Robert G. Benson

For over three thousand years, the Chinese have placed great value on the *I Ching*—also called the "Classic of Changes" and the "Book of Changes"—turning to it for guidance and insight. The *I Ching* is based on the deep understanding that our lives go through definable patterns, which can be determined by "consulting the Oracle"—the book of *I Ching*. Throughout the centuries, *I Ching* devotees have used the book as a means of understanding past, present, and future events, as well as exercising control over some events. The book highlights hundreds of different possibilities we might face in daily life, both on a professional and on a personal level.

For over ten years, researcher Robert Benson worked towards making the English text of the *I Ching* easier to understand and use. The result is a book that focuses on the text's essential meaning and is highly accessible to the modern Western reader. In addition, Benson provides an illuminating history of the *I Ching*, explaining how the text was created, discussing how it works, and exploring its many mysteries. Here is an *I Ching* that stands alone, providing a book of answers for anyone who faces a time of personal crisis and change.

$17.95 • 352 pages • 5.5 x 8.5-inch quality paperback • 2-color • Spiritualism/Chinese • ISBN 0-7570-0019-3

AS A MAN DOES
Morning and Evening Thoughts
James Allen

One of the first great modern writers of motivational and inspirational books, James Allen has influenced millions of people around the world through books like *As a Man Thinketh*. In the same way, *As a Man Does: Morning and Evening Thoughts* presents beautiful and insightful meditations to feed the mind and soul.

In each of the sixty-two meditations—one for each morning and each evening of the month—Allen offers both the force of truth and the blessing of comfort. Whether you are familiar with the writings of James Allen or you have yet to read any of his stirring books, this beautiful volume is sure to move you, console you, and inspire you—every morning and every evening of your life.

$8.95 • 96 pages • 5.5 x 8.5-inch quality paperback • 2-color • Inspiration/Religion • ISBN 0-7570-0018-5

THE NEW REVELATION
My Personal Investigation of Spiritualism
Sir Arthur Conan Doyle

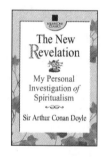

The spiritual movement in the early part of the twentieth century had few proponents greater than Sir Arthur Conan Doyle—a medical doctor, soldier, intellect, and world-renowned author of the Sherlock Holmes series. In 1918, Doyle published *The New Revelation*—a firsthand account of his personal investigation into the world of Spiritualism, which embraced areas that we refer to today as ESP, New Age philosophy, metaphysics, and psychic experiences. While some may view this work as a historical footnote, the answers to Sir Arthur's basic questions about life and death are as relevant today as they were then.

An original Introduction to the book by Dr. George J. Lankevich provides an insightful look at Doyle's personal life, and his friendship with magician Harry Houdini is brilliantly captured in an original Afterword.

$12.95 • 148 pages • 5.5 x 8.5-inch quality paperback • 2-color • Metaphysics • ISBN 0-7570-0017-7